1269 23×17 9432

The Giant Bathroom Book of Cartoons

The Giant Bathroom Book of Cartoons

Magpie Books, London

Constable & Robinson Ltd
3 The Lanchesters
162 Fulham Palace Road
London W6 9ER
www.constablerobinson.com

This edition published by Magpie Books, an
imprint of Constable & Robinson Ltd 2009

A copy of the British Library Cataloguing in
Publication Data is available from the British Library

ISBN 978-1-84901-211-9

Printed and bound in the EU

1 3 5 7 9 10 8 6 4 2

Contents

Animals

Cats are under tremendous
peer pressure to remain useless.

"It's because I'm a bull, isn't it".

Animals

"Well, it's similar to bungee jumping, but you go up instead of down."

Animals

"I don't like the way that rhino's
preparing to charge !"

6

"Let's see if you qualify for a handout.
How many nuts do you have currently,
and where are they buried?"

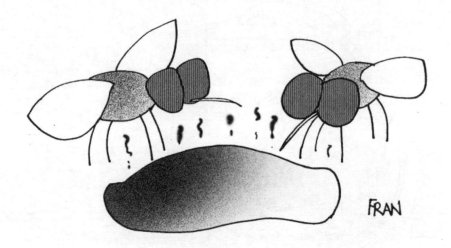

HEY MAN, THIS IS GOOD SHIT!

"Very funny - now can you spit the water back out"

Animals

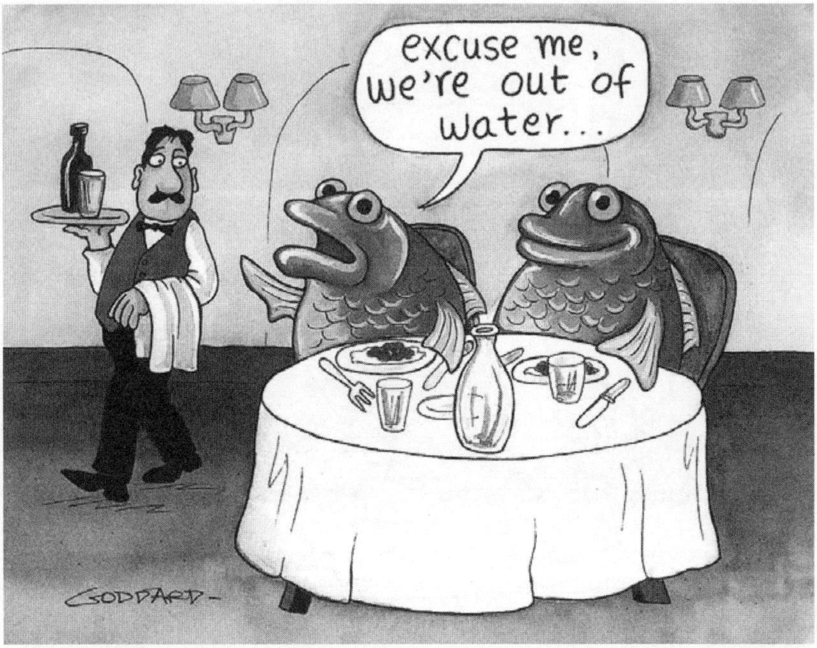
excuse me, we're out of water...
GODDARD

"Sure, I'm calmer. I'm just concerned the tranquilizer darts may be habit-forming."

Animals

'Vultures are renowned for their use of thermals'.

Big dogs. One of the reasons
little dogs are so nervous.

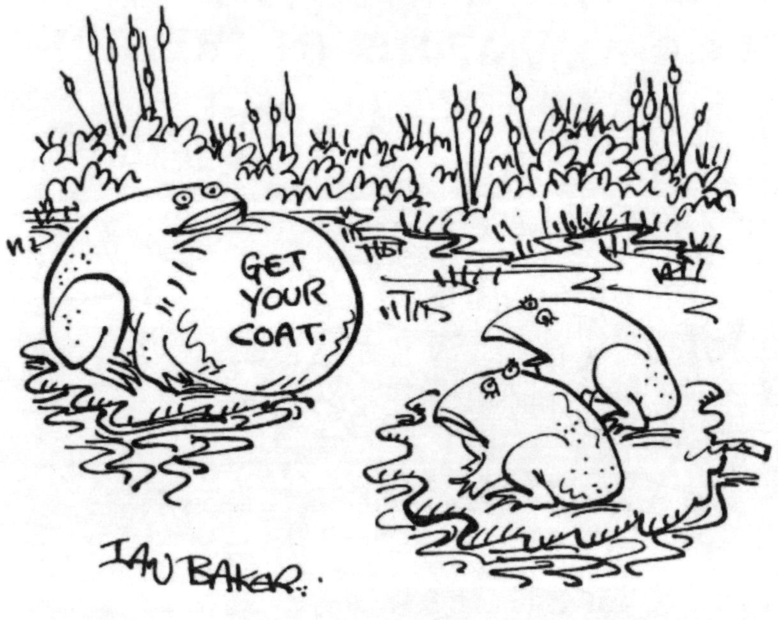
GET
YOUR
COAT.
IAN BAKER

"I think he likes you."

Animals

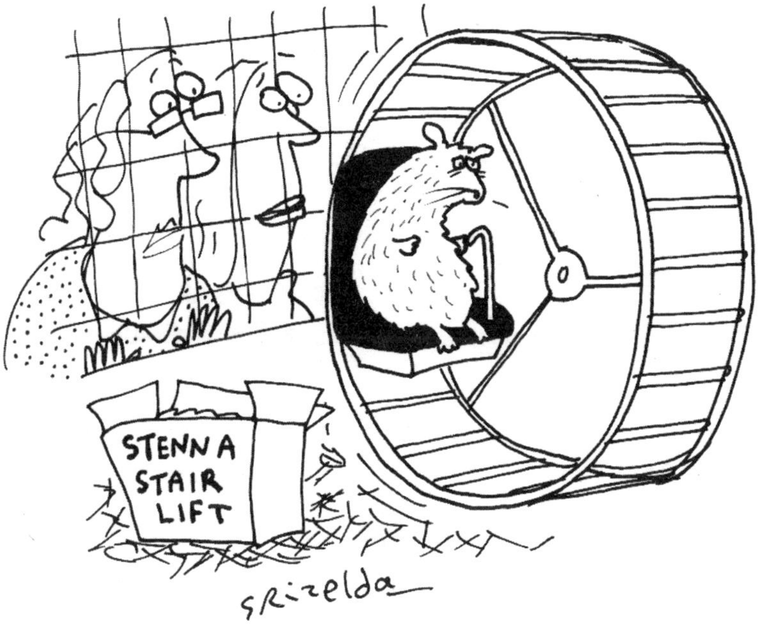

STENNA
STAIR
LIFT
GRIZELDA

Animals

"Mum, Dad. This is Sushi."

INSULT

OF THE DAY

I have had a perfectly wonderful evening, but this wasn't it.

GROUCHO MARX

JOKE OF THE DAY

Two cows were talking in a field one day.
   The first cow said: 'Have you heard the one about the Mad Cow Disease that's going around?'
   The second cow said: 'Yeah, makes you glad you're a penguin, doesn't it?'

Art

"For goodness sake Miss Pendleton,
stop jiggling about!"

Art

"It's fabulous! I'll give you £25,000 for it!"

Art

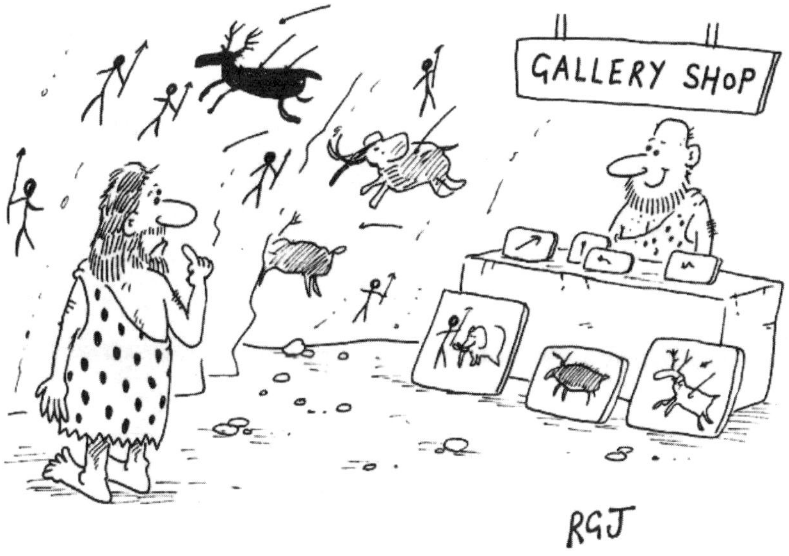
GALLERY SHOP
RGJ

"I'm sorry Miss, but your artistic license has expired."

Art

"Err... The exhibits are this way dear."

Art

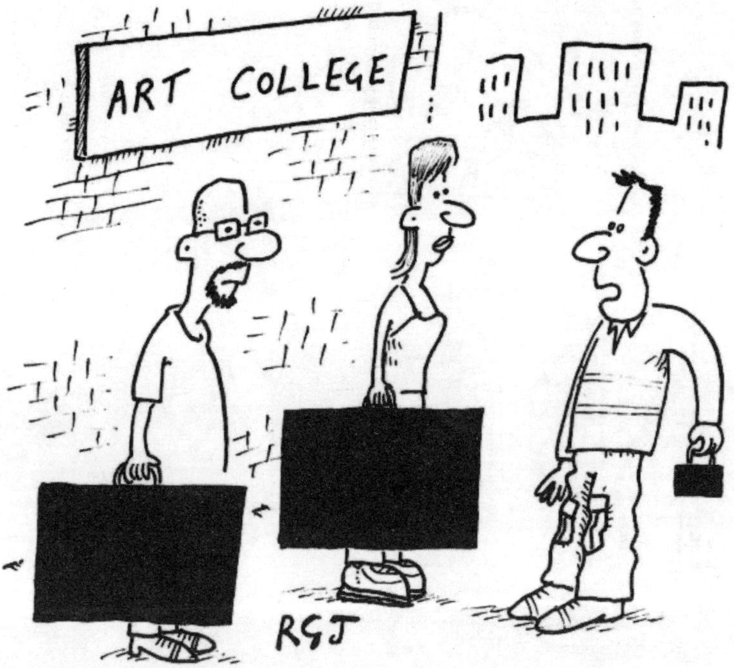
ART COLLEGE
RGJ

"I'm a minimalist."

Art

"We have yellow ochre, but no mediocre.
Maybe you misunderstood the teacher."

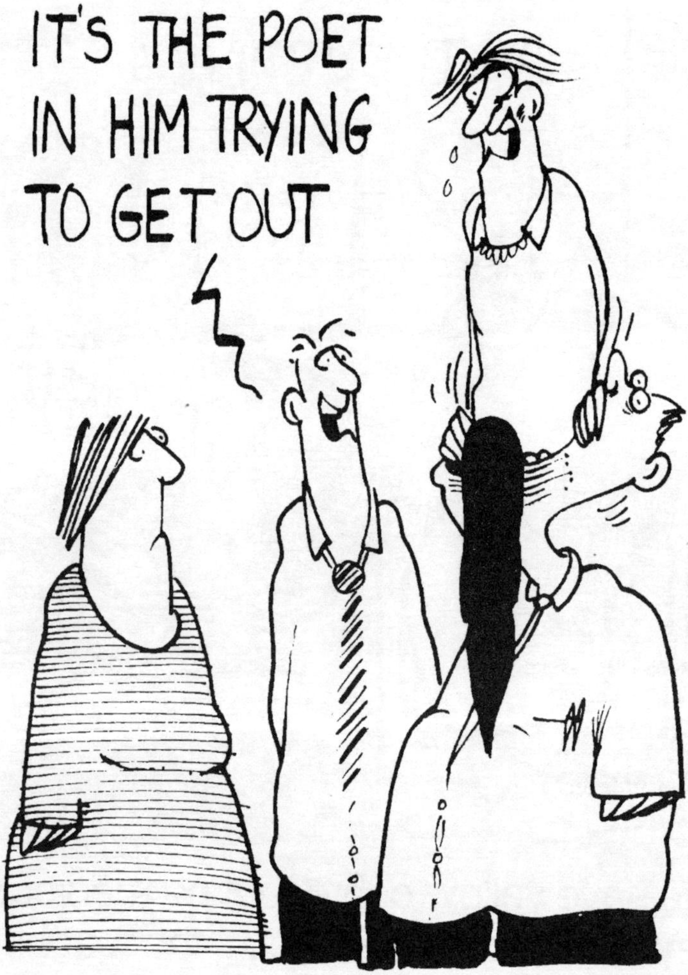
IT'S THE POET IN HIM TRYING TO GET OUT

Art

"An art forger? How dare you! I am an Henri Matisse tribute act!"

Art

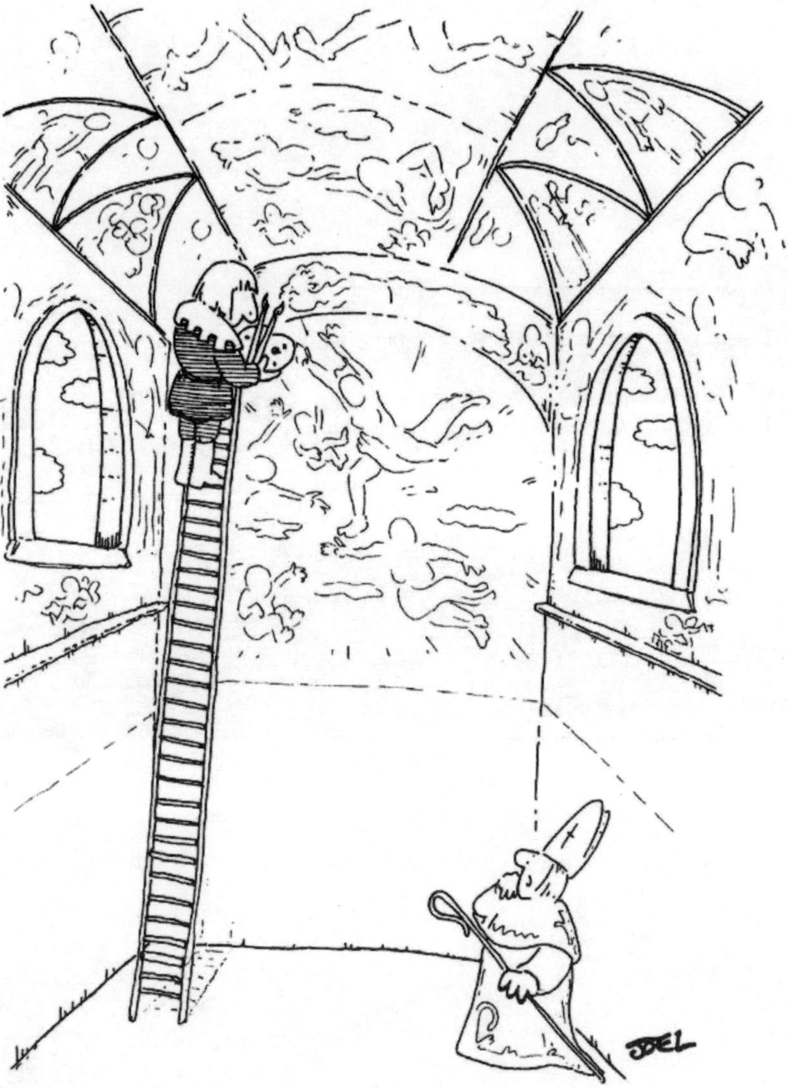
JOEL

..but is it art ?

THOUGHT
FOR THE DAY

If a man is standing in the middle of the forest speaking and there is no woman around to hear him, is he still wrong?

INSULT
OF THE DAY

Any similarity between him and a human being is entirely coincidental.

Business and Work

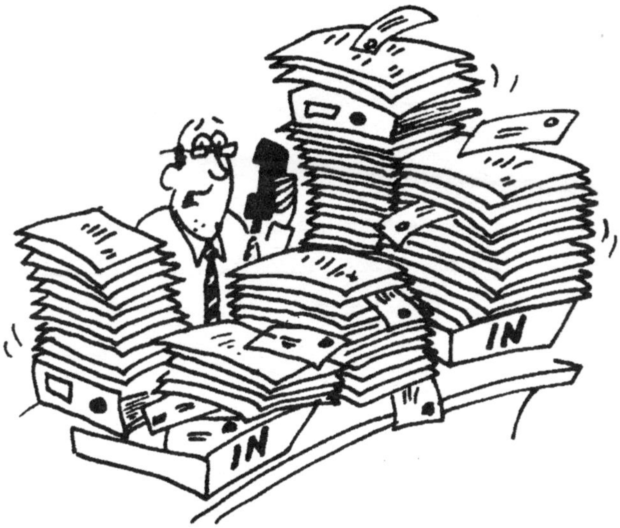
IN
IN

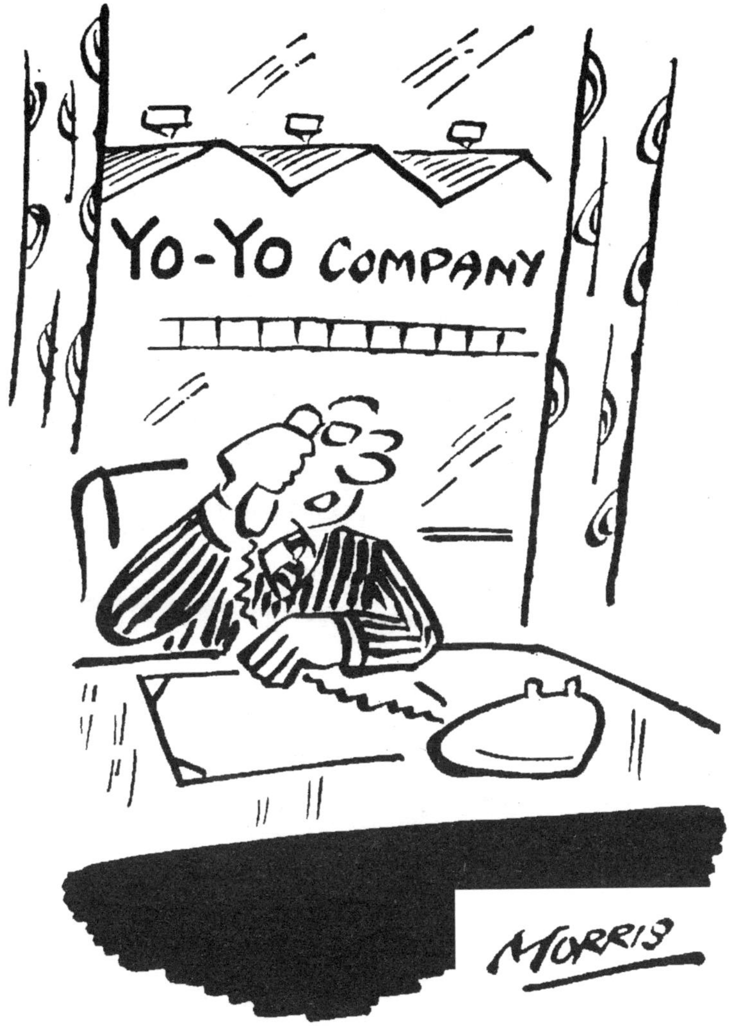
YO-YO COMPANY
MORRIS

"Business is up and down."

Business and Work

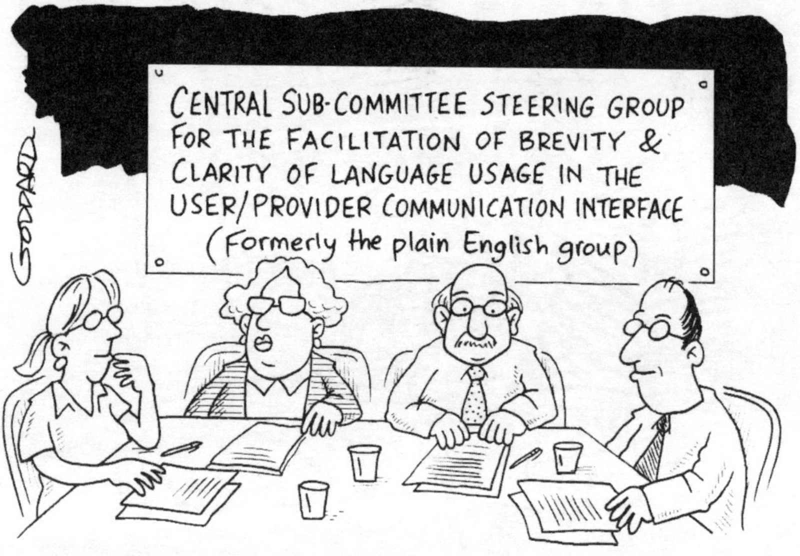
CENTRAL SUB-COMMITTEE STEERING GROUP
FOR THE FACILITATION OF BREVITY &
CLARITY OF LANGUAGE USAGE IN THE
USER/PROVIDER COMMUNICATION INTERFACE
(Formerly the plain English group)
GODDARD

"Yes, I have your letter on my desk in front of me."

Business and Work

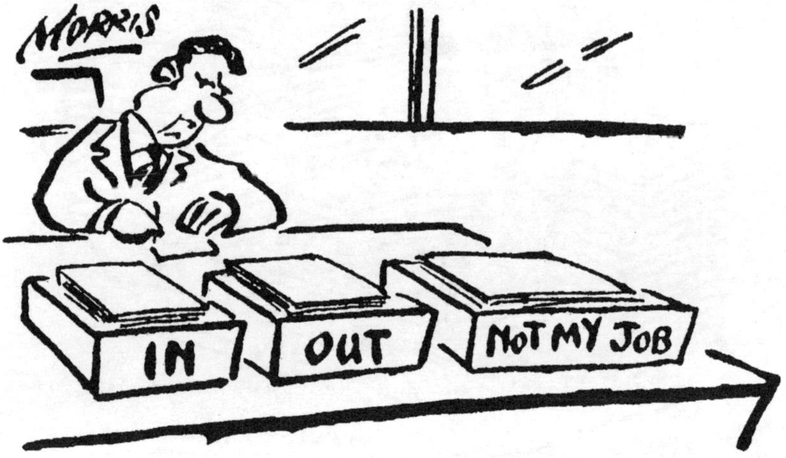
MORRIS
IN
OUT
NOT MY JOB

THE CHRISTMAS PARTY IS CANCELLED, BUT
AS A COMPROMISE YOU CAN STILL COME
IN AND HAVE SEX IN THE STATIONERY
CUPBOARD

Business and Work

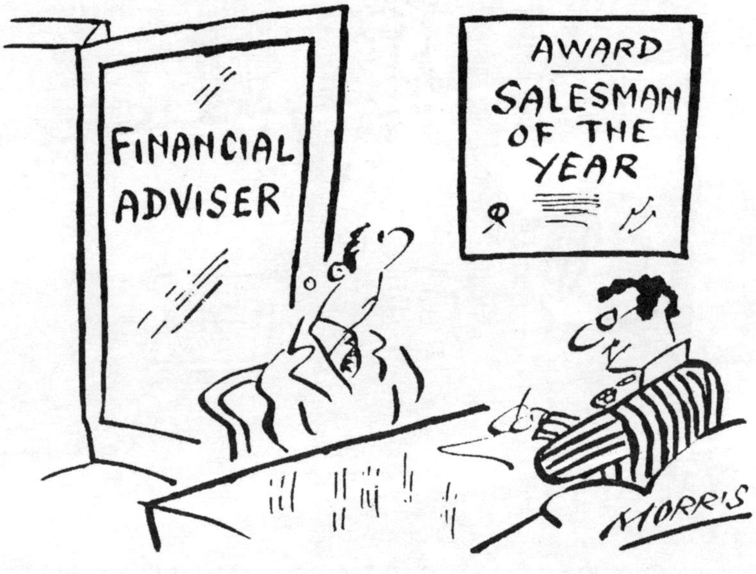
FINANCIAL ADVISER
AWARD
SALESMAN OF THE YEAR
MORRIS

Business and Work

"You win some, you lose some. Don't worry about it. No one's keeping score."

41

"WE'VE SAVED A FORTUNE RELOCATING OUR CHILDREN TO ASIA..."

"If at first you don't succeed is not
company policy, Anderson!"

"Look, I said I'd bring you the report on micromanaging. Just give me a chance."

Business and Work

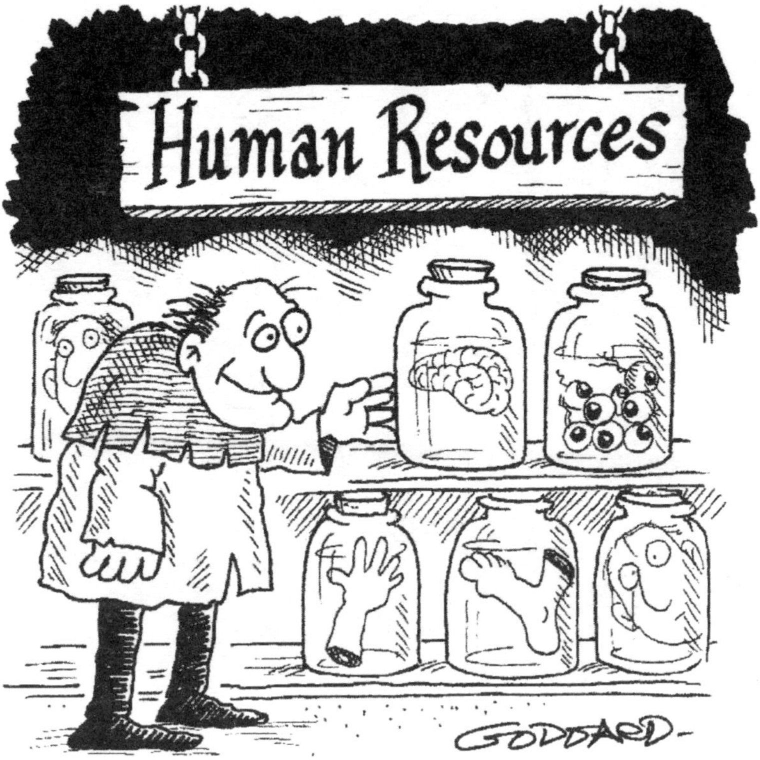
Human Resources
GODDARD

Business and Work

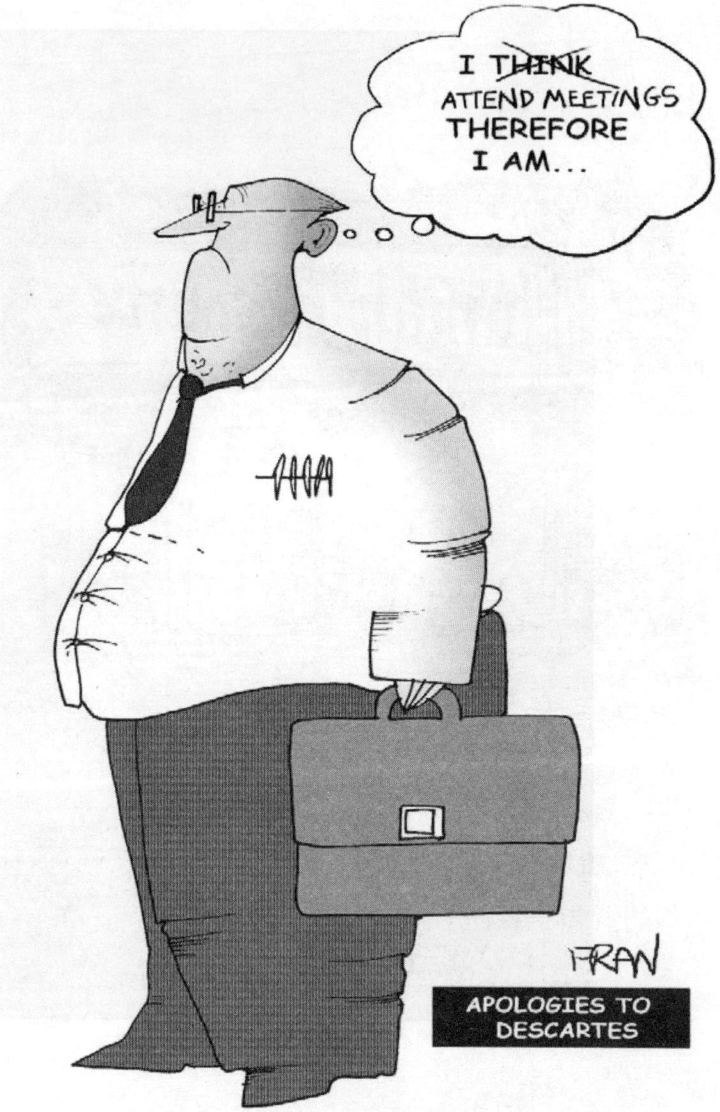
I THINK
ATTEND MEETINGS
THEREFORE
I AM...
FRAN
APOLOGIES TO
DESCARTES

"We'll skip that rubbish."

Business and Work

"Isn't that a surveillance camera?"

"Do you ever worry you've had to sacrifice your femininity to succeed in the male business world."

JOKE OF THE DAY

A small boy came home from school and told his father excitedly: 'I've been given a part in the school play.'

'That's great, son. Who are you playing?'

'The husband.'

Dad frowned. 'Go back and tell your teacher you want a speaking part.'

THOUGHT
FOR THE DAY

How is it that 'fat chance'
and 'slim chance' mean the
same thing?

INSULT

OF THE DAY

She's the original good time that was had by all.

BETTE DAVIS

Children

"It's nice to see the police toughening up on juvenile crime"

Children

"I'm afraid our worst suspicions have been confirmed -
We found slug, snail and a trace amount of puppydog tail."

Children

"Only twenty-five kids? Have you considered
fertility treatment?"

" One day all this will be chores."

Children

Children

"Stop kicking the back of my chair!"

Children

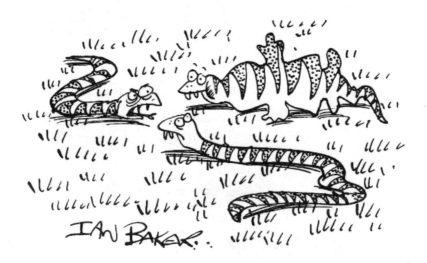

"Alright. Who had the last toddler?"

61

Children

"One day, this will all be your fault."

Children

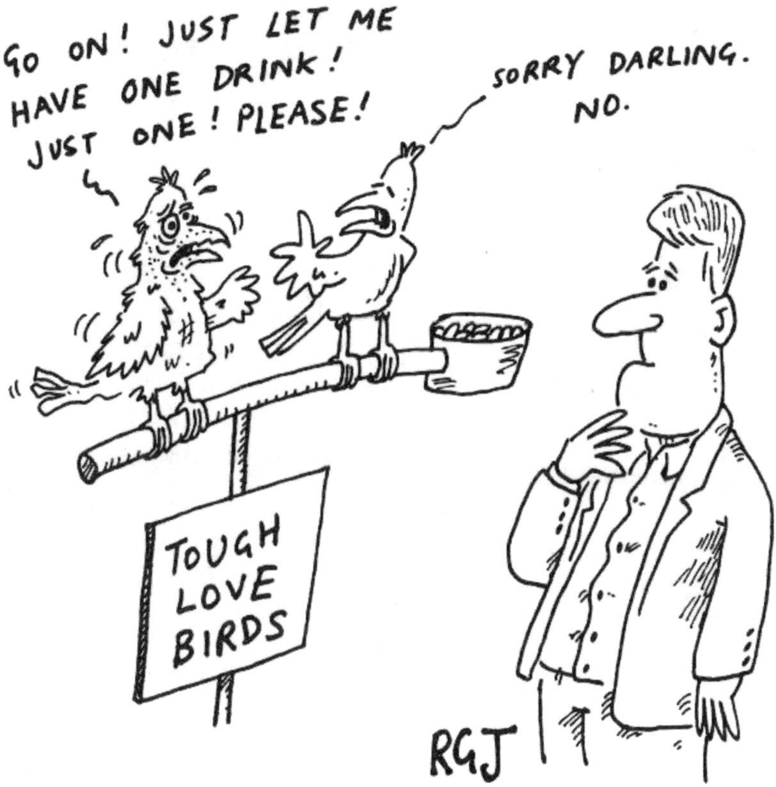
GO ON! JUST LET ME HAVE ONE DRINK! JUST ONE! PLEASE!
SORRY DARLING. NO.
TOUGH LOVE BIRDS
RGJ

Children

"Of course Daddy & I don't mind you pillow
fighting. As long as you wear your goverment
approved pillow fighting, helmet, goggles & pads."

JOKE OF THE DAY

A banker fell overboard while taking a cruise on a friend's yacht. The friend grabbed a lifebelt, held it up, and, not knowing if the banker could swim, shouted: 'Can you float alone?'

'Of course I can! yelled the banker. 'But this is a heck of a time to talk business!'

THOUGHT
FOR THE DAY

Work keeps us from three great evils: boredom, vice and need.

VOLTAIRE

Christmas

Christmas

"Hello, is that the temp agency? Now listen,
I specifically asked for *Elves!*"

"I agreed to guide you. My contract says nothing about pulling a sleigh."

Christmas

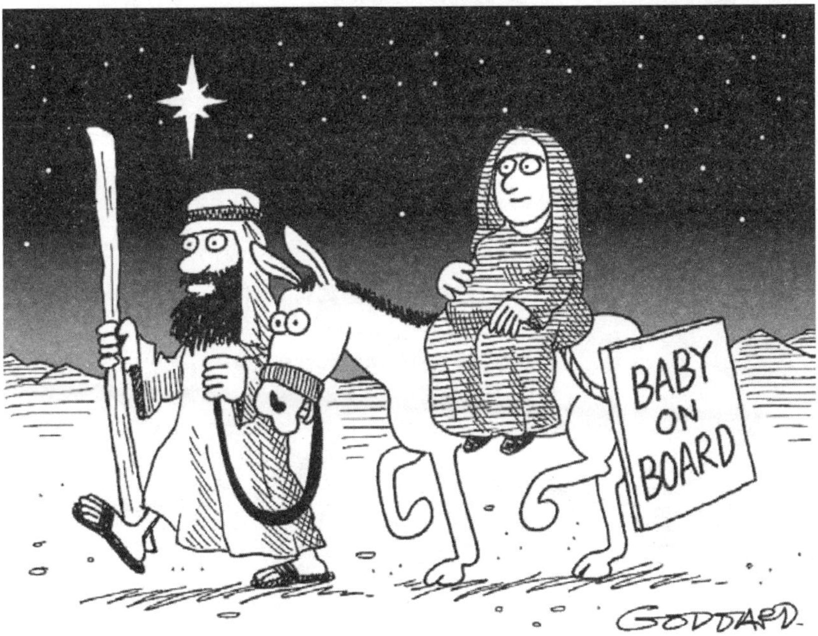
BABY
ON
BOARD
GODDARD

Christmas

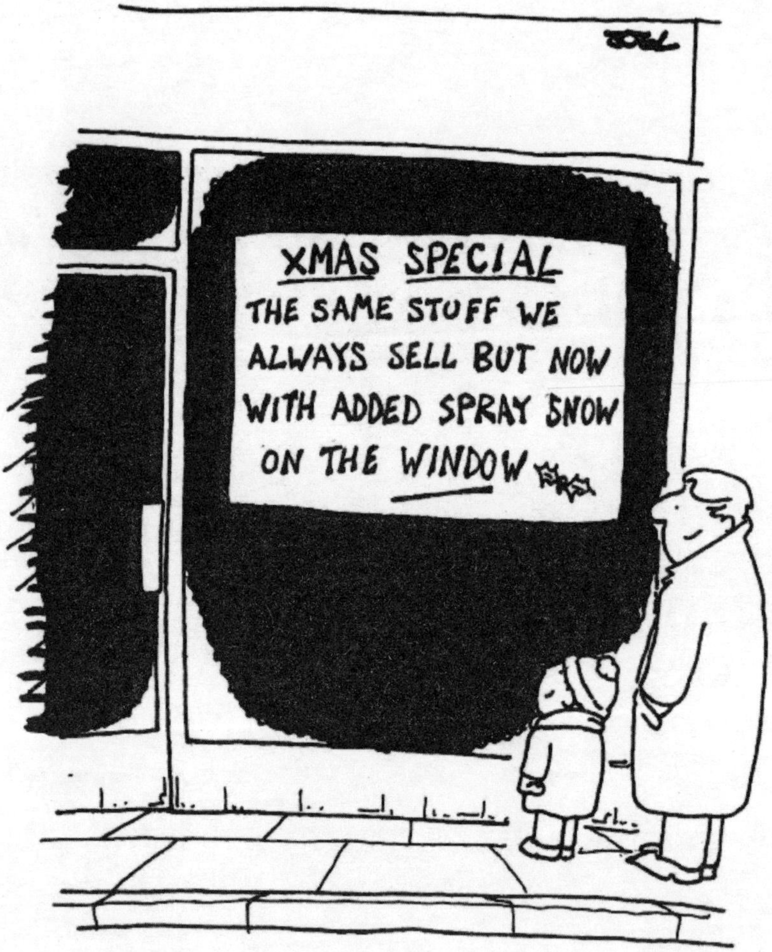
XMAS SPECIAL
THE SAME STUFF WE
ALWAYS SELL BUT NOW
WITH ADDED SPRAY SNOW
ON THE WINDOW

Death and Funerals

"Ashes to ashes, dust to dust,
bowl to bowl."

Christmas

IT'S THE GHOST OF CHRISTMAS PRESENT

Christmas

'FOR GOODNESS SAKE! SLOW DOWN AND WATCH
WHERE YOU'RE GOING...'

Christmas

"and I suppose you'll be working again this Christmas?"

"So I thought why bother buying lots of small ones.."

Christmas

INSULT
OF THE DAY

Before he came along we
were hungry. Now we are
fed up.

Computers

MODERN POST

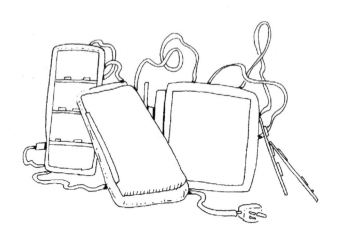

POST MODERN

LOSER'S GUIDE TO ONLINE TRADING

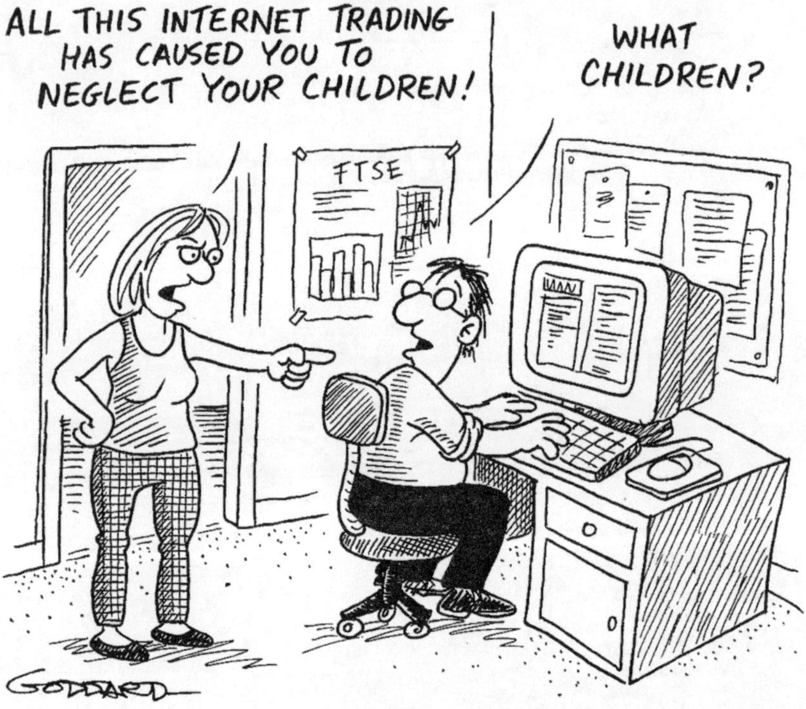
ALL THIS INTERNET TRADING HAS CAUSED YOU TO NEGLECT YOUR CHILDREN!
WHAT CHILDREN?
FTSE
GODDARD

Computers

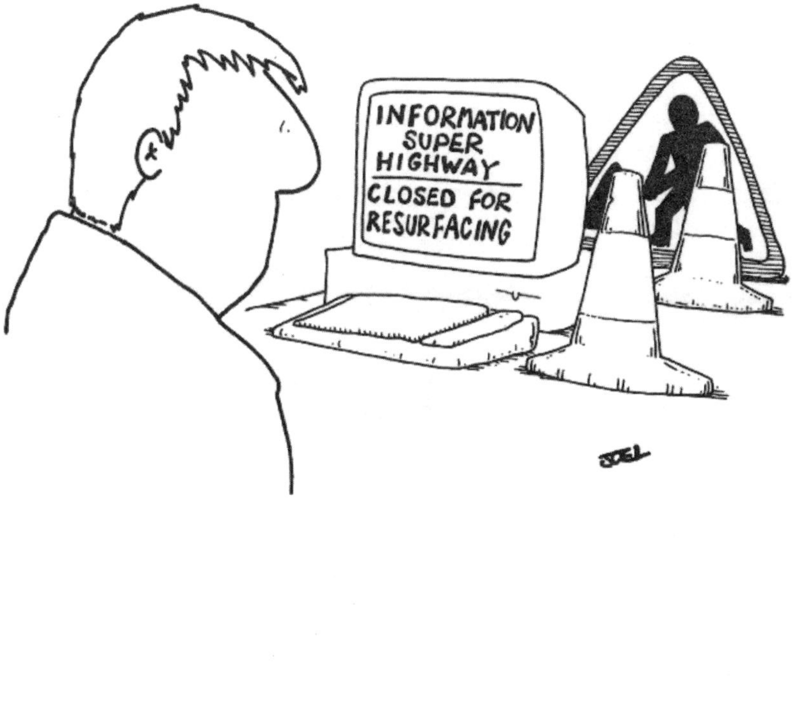
INFORMATION
SUPER
HIGHWAY
CLOSED FOR
RESURFACING
JOEL

Computers

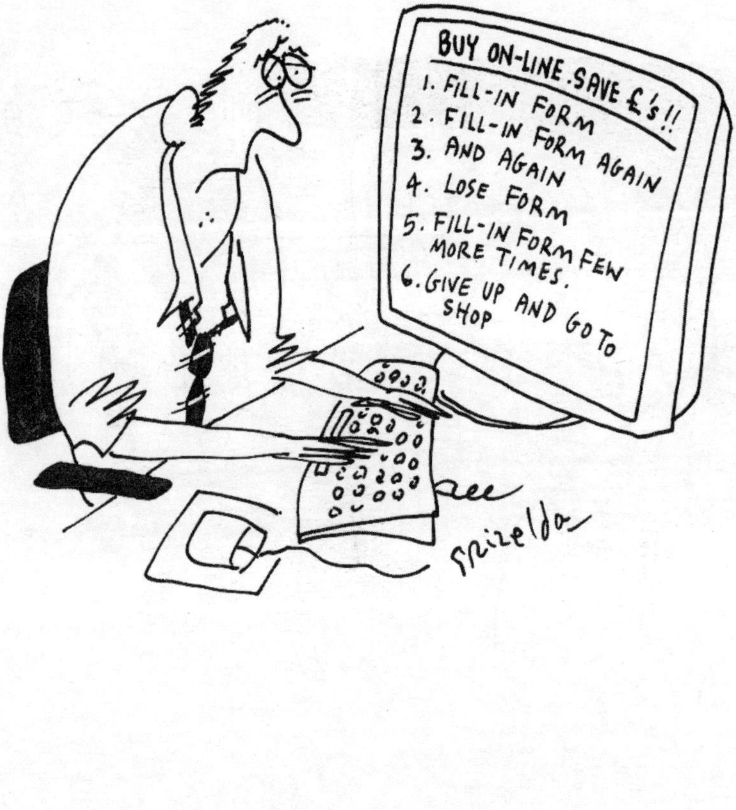
BUY ON-LINE. SAVE £'s!!
1. FILL-IN FORM
2. FILL-IN FORM AGAIN
3. AND AGAIN
4. LOSE FORM
5. FILL-IN FORM FEW MORE TIMES.
6. GIVE UP AND GO TO SHOP
Grizelda

Computers

The e-merchant of Venice

Computers

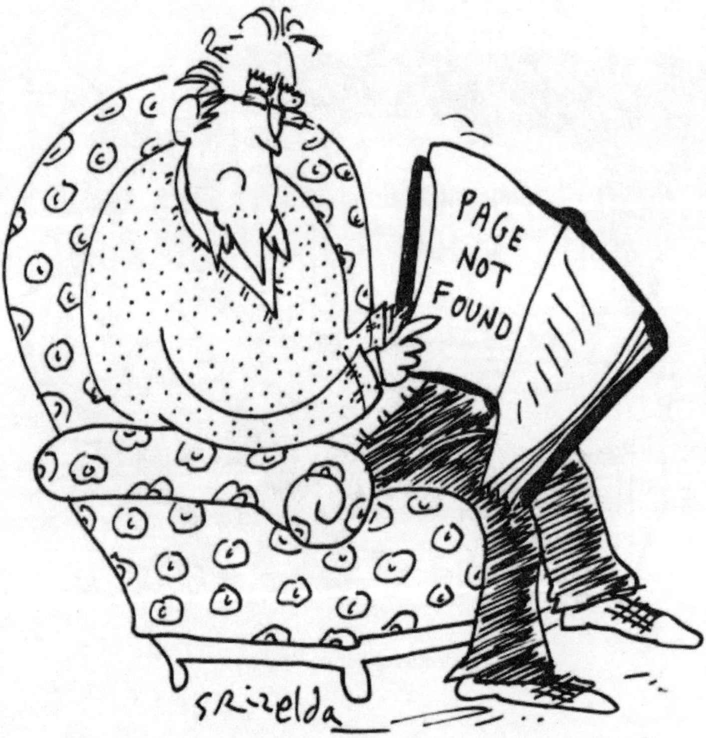
PAGE
NOT
FOUND

'I think the computer's trying to download
something.'

"Like, hello… nothing's wrong with the software. You hit delete. If you want to answer prayers, hit send."

Computers

'YOU'VE COPIED ALL THIS OFF
THE INTERNET...'

INSULT
OF THE DAY

He has delusions of adequacy.

90

Death and Funerals

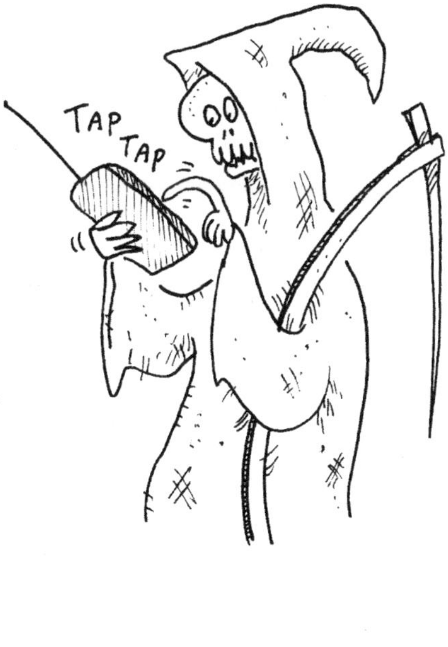
TAP TAP

Death and Funerals

"I think he must have had a death wish."

93

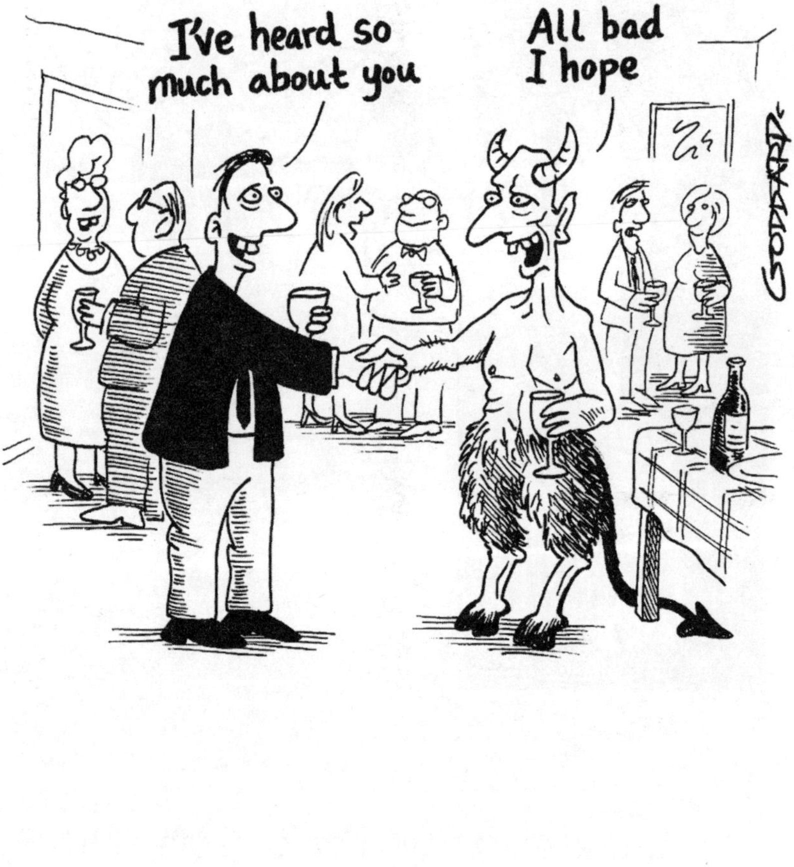
I've heard so much about you
All bad I hope
GODDARD

Death and Funerals

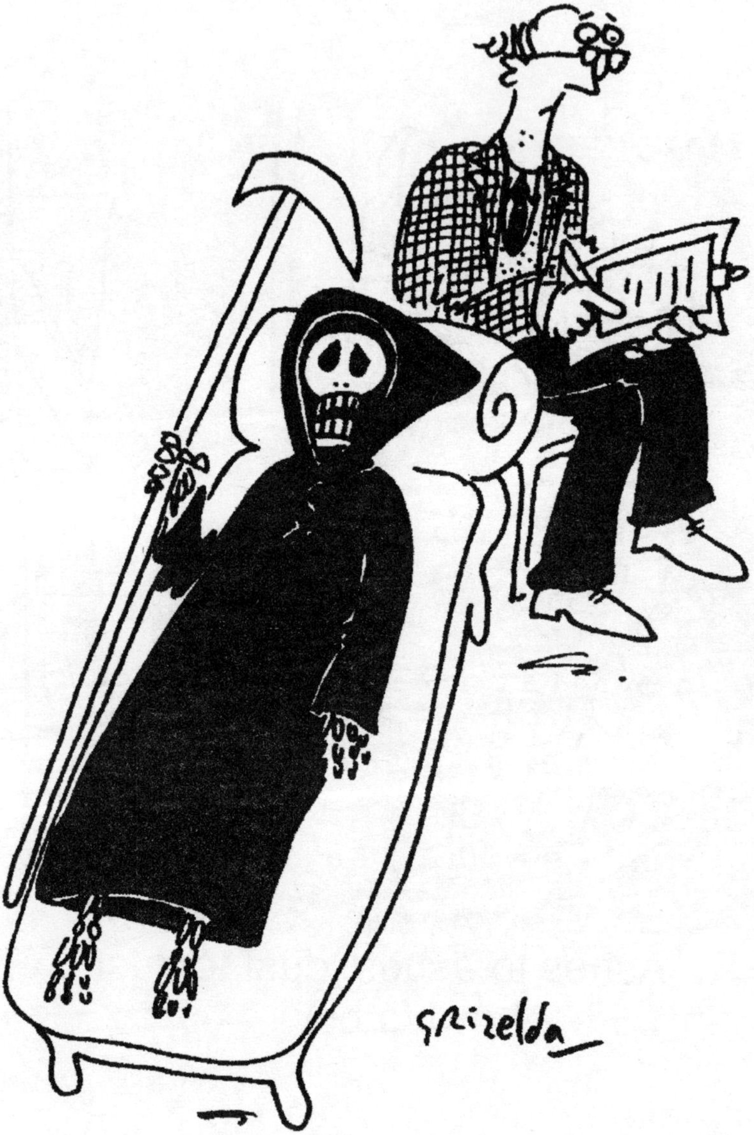
GRIZELDA

Death and Funerals

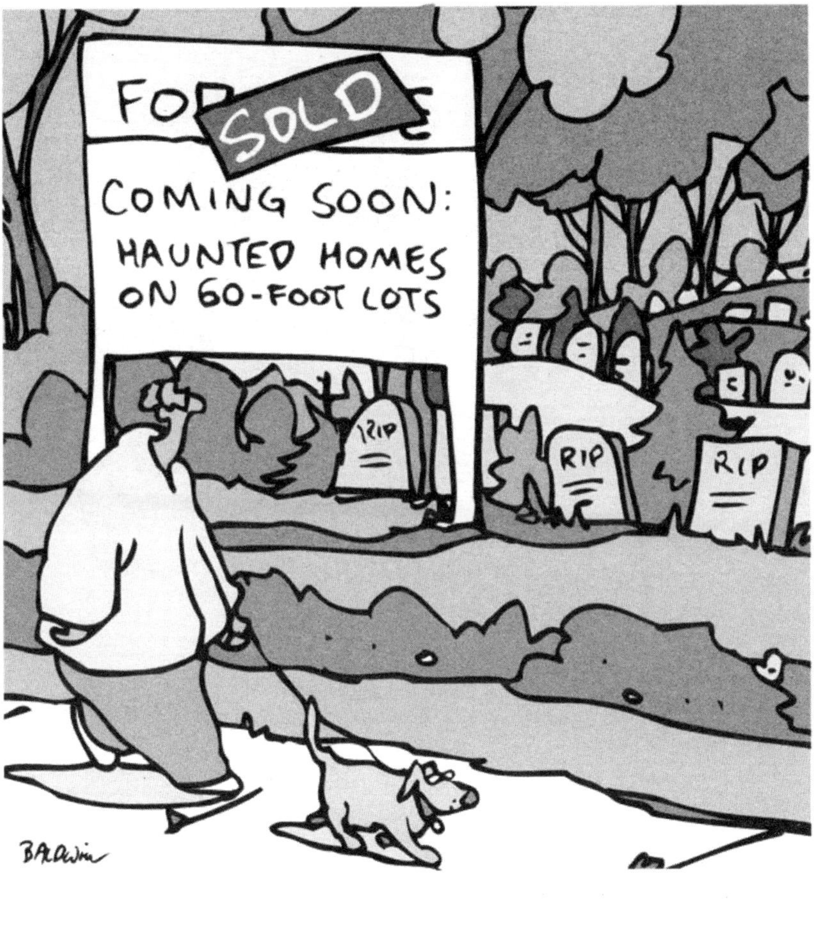

FOR SOLD
COMING SOON:
HAUNTED HOMES
ON 60-FOOT LOTS
RIP
RIP
RIP
BALDWIN

Death and Funerals

Death in Venice

"Actually, I'm still on life support.
I just came by to do a feasibility study."

Death and Funerals

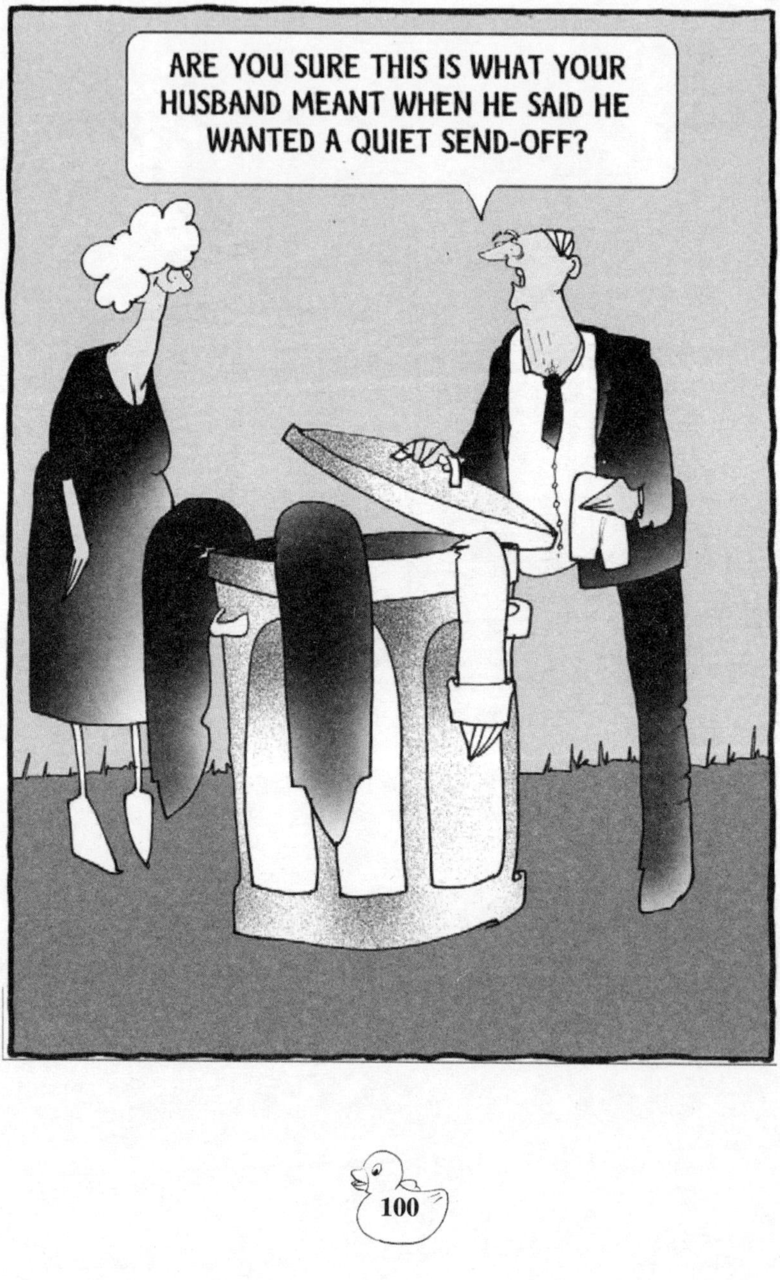
ARE YOU SURE THIS IS WHAT YOUR HUSBAND MEANT WHEN HE SAID HE WANTED A QUIET SEND-OFF?

Death and Funerals

"Welcome. You're in either heaven or hell, depending on your sex."

Death and Funerals

"Was that the tea trolley or a death rattle?"

102

Death and Funerals

"Not to worry. If I remember correctly, the sign described it as, 'death-defying.'"

Death and Funerals

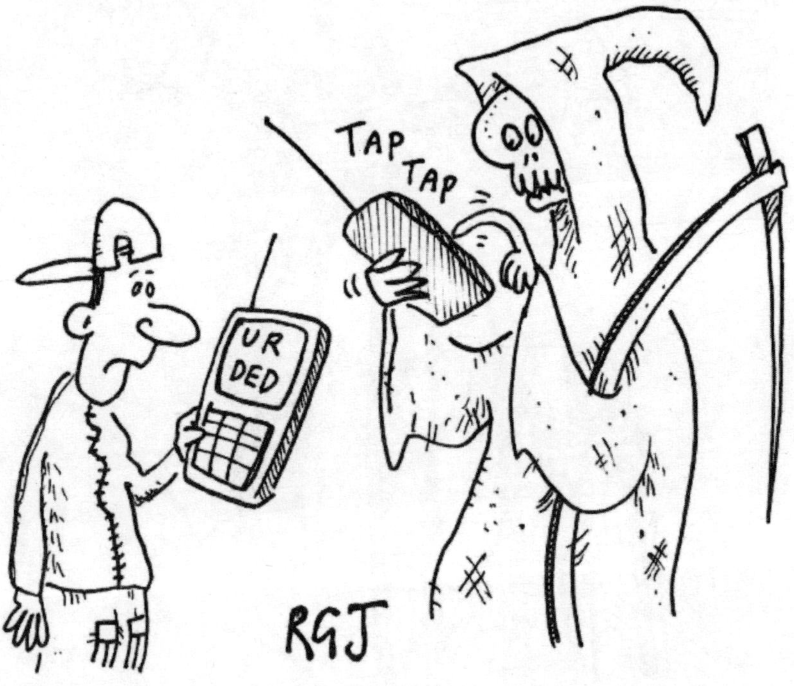
TAP TAP
UR DED
RGJ

Death and Funerals

"It's a crying shame - his wife went to visit her mother in Australia and forgot to leave directions to the kitchen"

JOKE OF THE DAY

Did you hear about the boy who sat under a cow? He got a pat on the head.

Family and Home

Family and Home

"I usually wait for it to stop spinning."

Family and Home

"Phew! I'm bushed! I've been up all night helping
the removal men clear the front room."

Family and Home

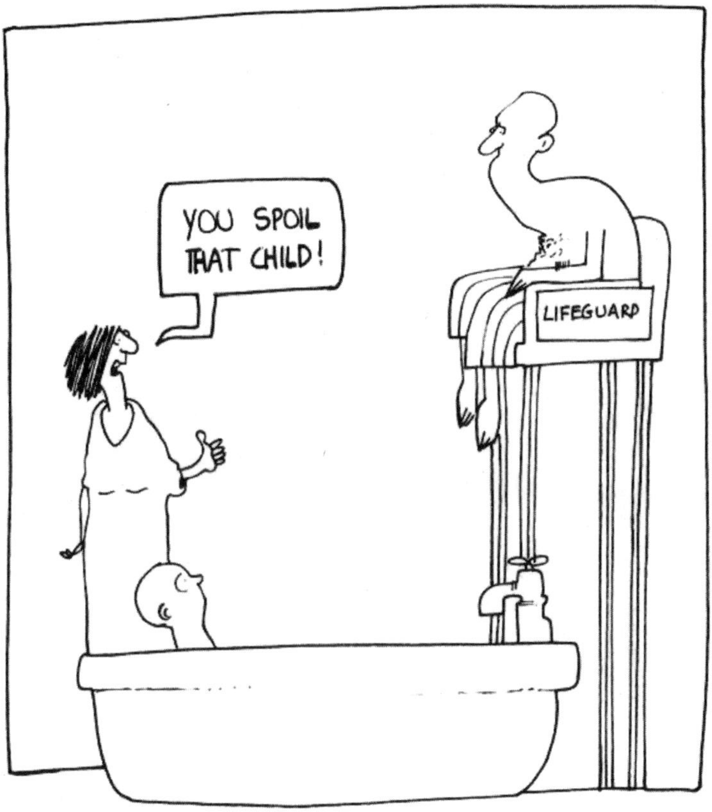
YOU SPOIL THAT CHILD!
LIFEGUARD

Family and Home

"Today I'd like to teach everyone the difficult task Of, how to put a new toilet roll on it's holder."

Family and Home

"How old do you think you have to be before you can visit you parents
and get treated like a grown-up?"

Family and Home

"Take no notice of her! Next time just fetch my slippers!"

Family and Home

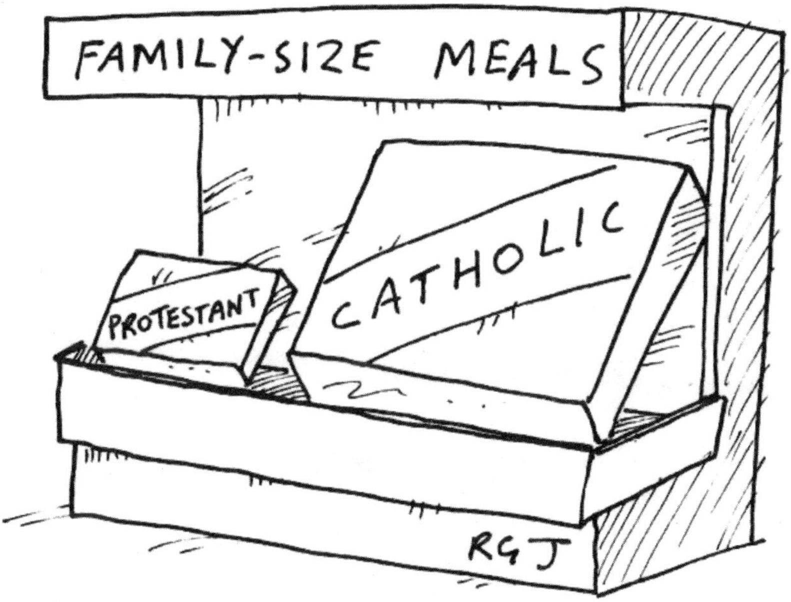

FAMILY-SIZE MEALS
PROTESTANT
CATHOLIC
RGJ

"Have you chosen your bedtime story yet Tommy?"

Family and Home

"Ah, Norman. This is Mr and Mrs Pembleton, they're going to be moving into the flat above us."

THOUGHT
FOR THE DAY

Failure is just the first step on the road to success . . . or wherever.

Fashion and Shopping

Fashion and Shopping

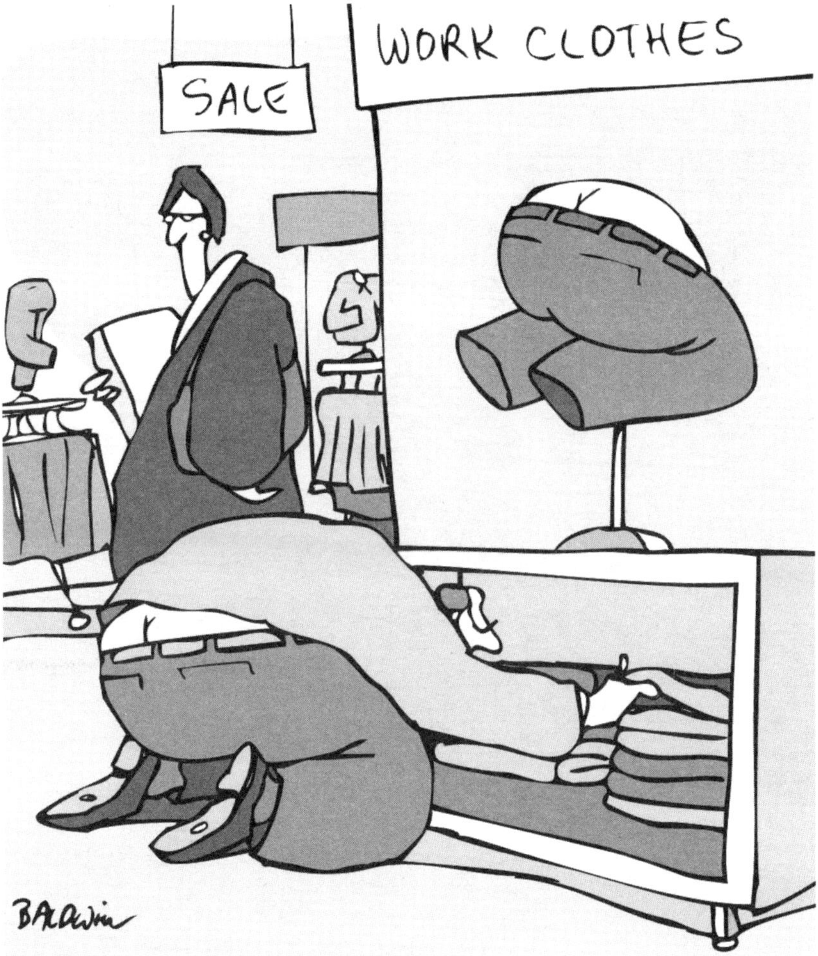
SALE
WORK CLOTHES
BALDWIN

Fashion and Shopping

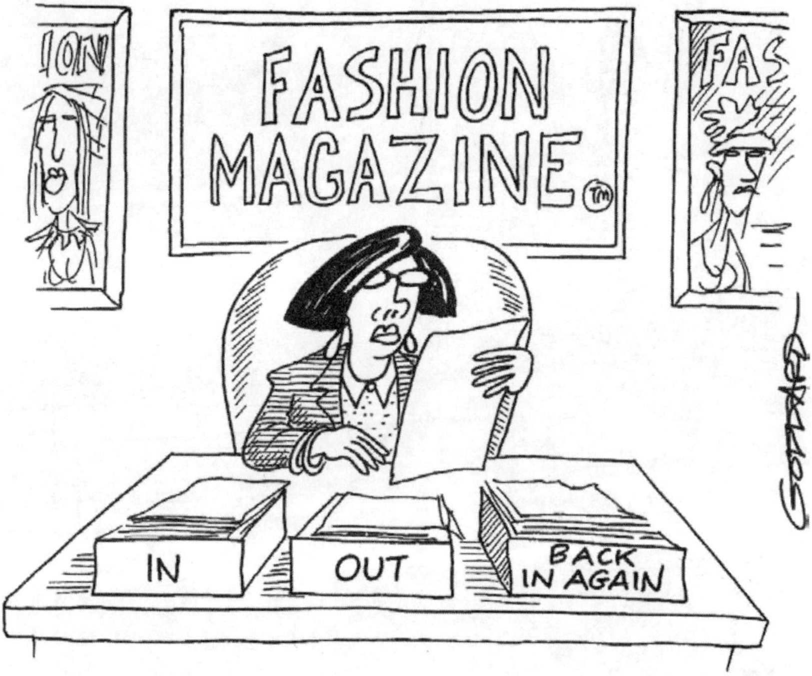
FASHION MAGAZINE
IN
OUT
BACK IN AGAIN

Fashion and Shopping

"The tide's getting ready to go out."

Fashion and Shopping

"Do these plants make me look fat?"

Fashion and Shopping

"I'll not have whatever you're not having !"

Fashion and Shopping

"Police clashed with protesters again today. Witnesses say the fabrics, textures and color schemes were just hideous."

Fashion and Shopping

"If your name's not down...."

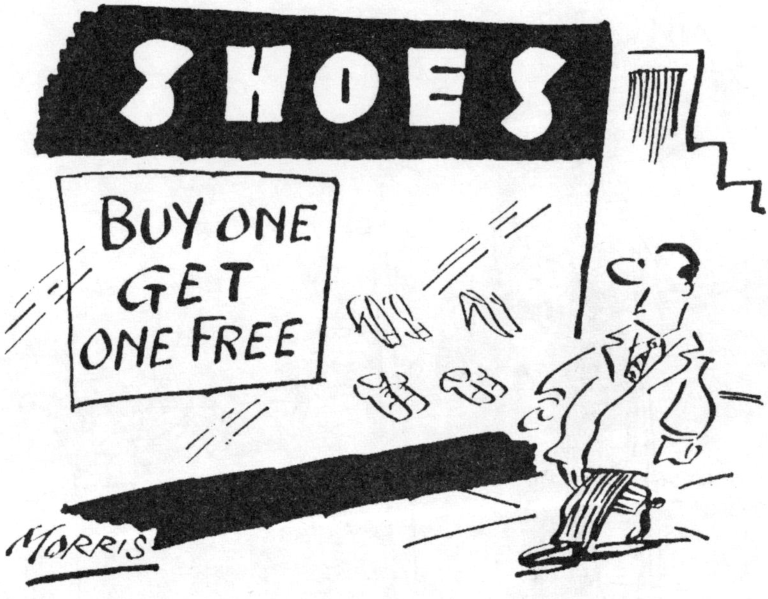
SHOES
BUY ONE
GET
ONE FREE
MORRIS

Fashion and Shopping

FASHION NURSERY SCHOOL

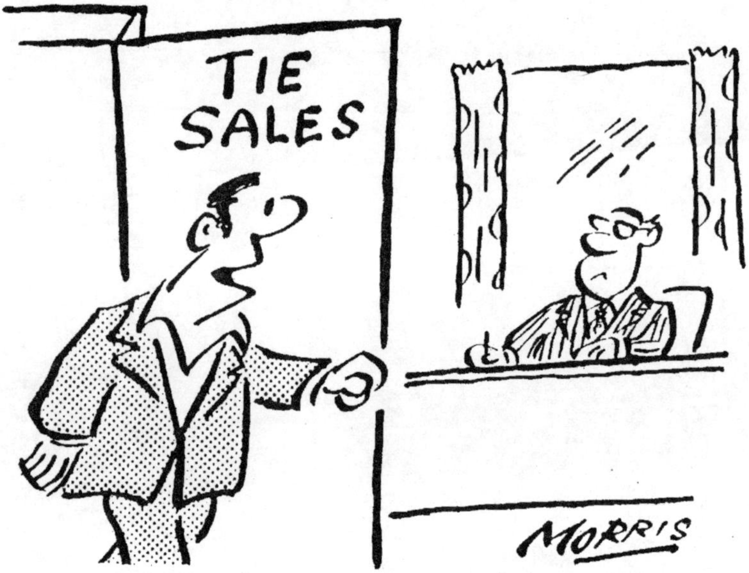
TIE
SALES
MORRIS

"You wished to see me, JB?"

INSULT
OF THE DAY

He has all the characteristics of a dog except loyalty.

JOKE OF THE DAY

If a train station is where a train stops
and a bus station is where a bus stops,
what's a work station?

Food and Drink

Food and Drink

"One cappuccino coming right up!"

Food and Drink

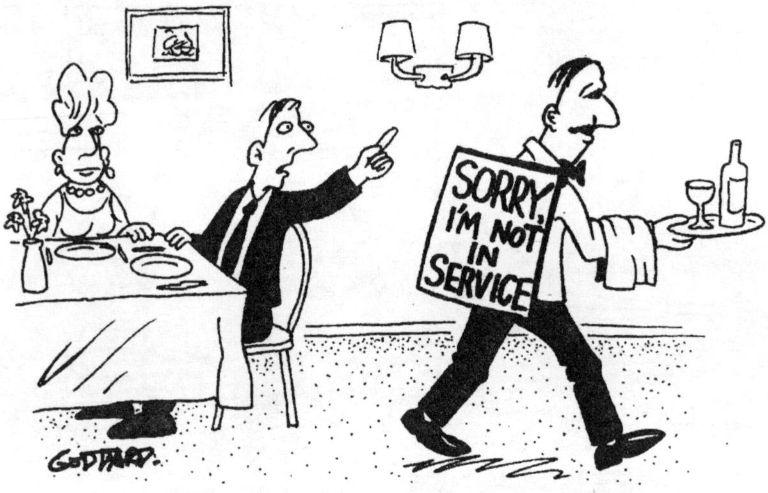
SORRY, I'M NOT IN SERVICE
GODDARD.

"Well Lucky, for starters, I think the horseshoe was a bad idea."

Food and Drink

"Well it doesn't look like a paperweight to
me, Harris."

Food and Drink

"Oh no! Vegelanties!"

Food and Drink

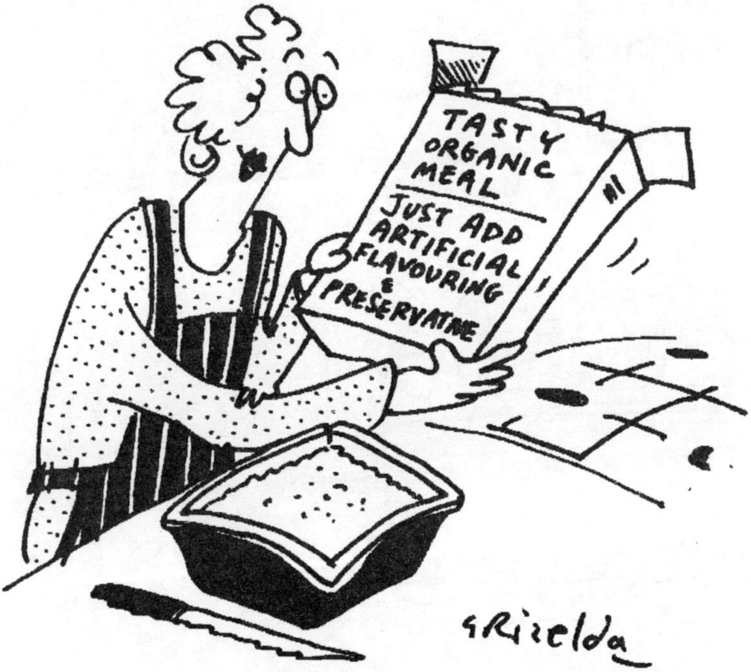
TASTY ORGANIC MEAL
JUST ADD ARTIFICIAL FLAVOURING & PRESERVATIVE
GRIZELDA

Food and Drink

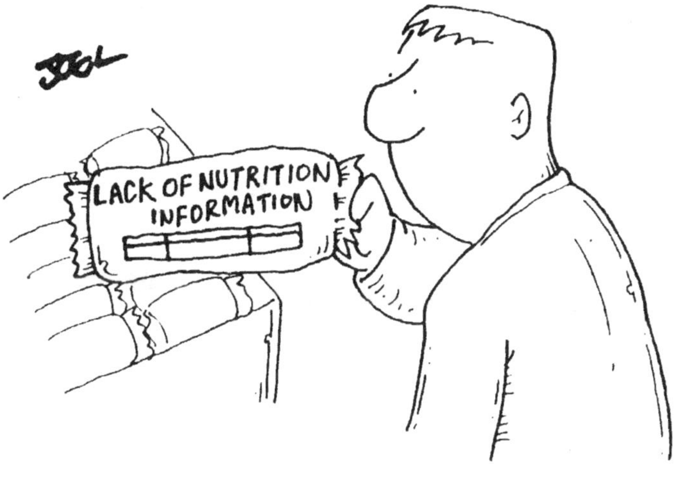
LACK OF NUTRITION INFORMATION

Food and Drink

'EXCELLENT! THIS CRAP AGAIN'

Food and Drink

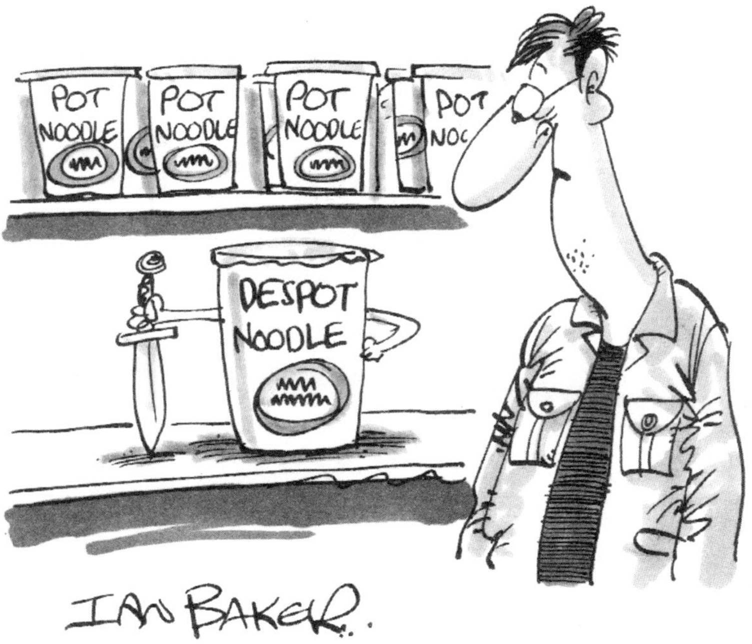

POT NOODLE
DESPOT NOODLE
IAN BAKER

Food and Drink

It isn't about what's right or wrong, but choosing what's right for you. Therapy makes shopping way more difficult.

THOUGHT
FOR THE DAY

The grass is always greener after ten days of relentless driving rain.

INSULT

OF THE DAY

He doesn't know the meaning of the word 'failure', but then again he doesn't know the meaning of most words.

Health and Beauty

Health and Beauty

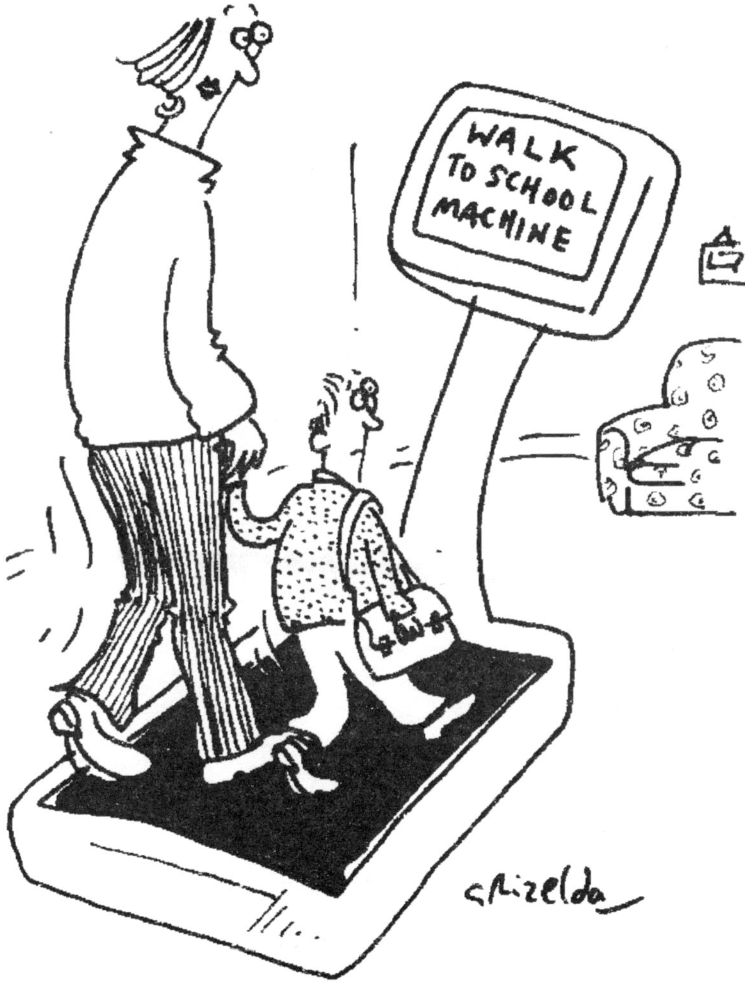
WALK TO SCHOOL MACHINE
Grizelda

Health and Beauty

"I shan't be in today - I'm in bed with a nasty bug".

Health and Beauty

SO THIS 'FLAMINGO DIET'...DOES IT WORK?

Health and Beauty

"Oh shit!"   "Ugh shfjittthh!"

Health and Beauty

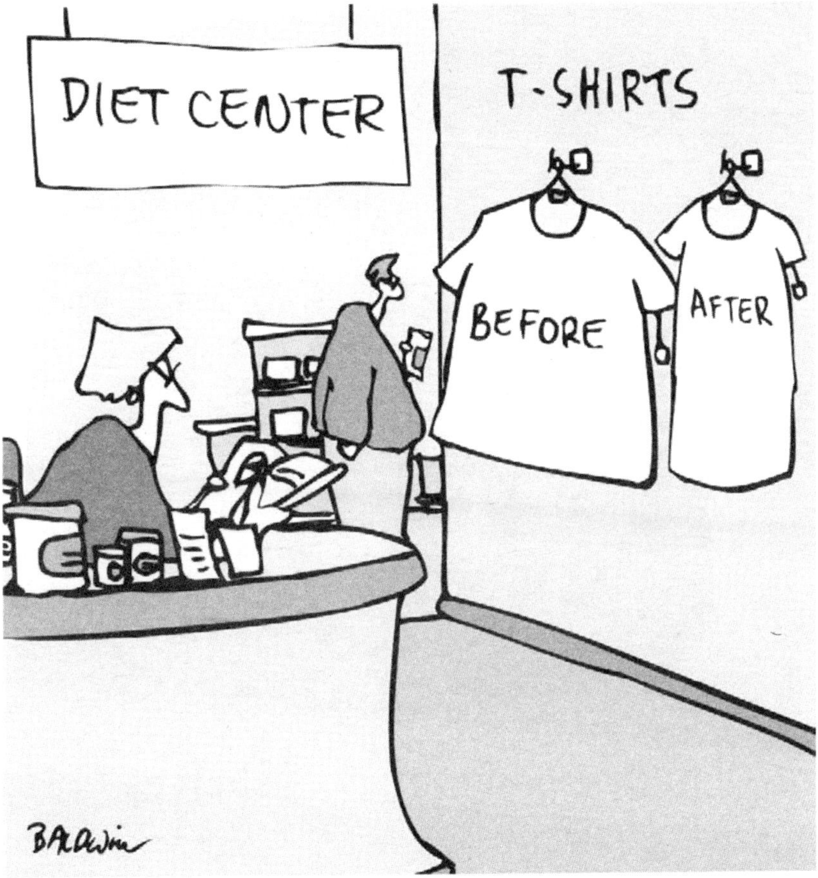
DIET CENTER
T-SHIRTS
BEFORE
AFTER
BALDWIN

"I'm de-toxing my bookshelves."

Health and Beauty

When he got the wrong medication, no one would own up to it. They were real good at covering their own butts.

Health and Beauty

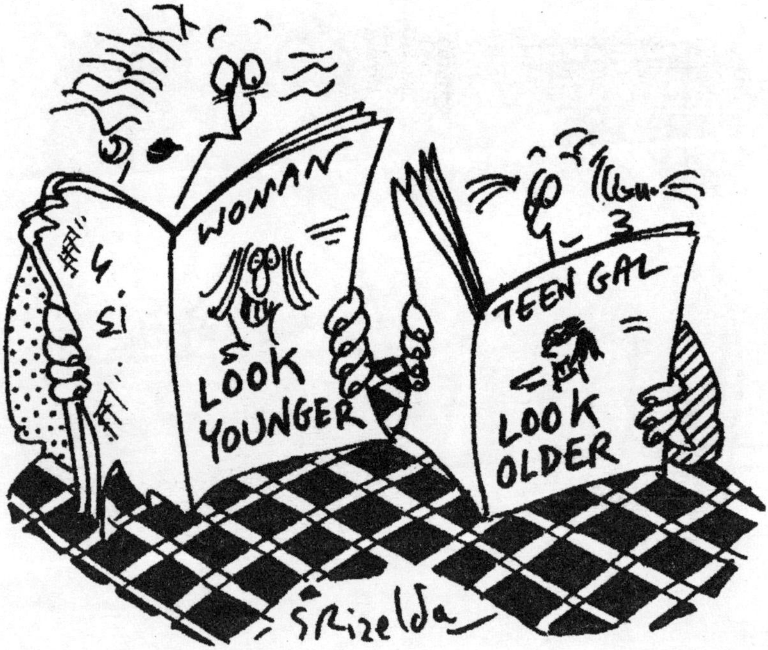
WOMAN
LOOK YOUNGER
TEEN GAL
LOOK OLDER
GRIZELDA

Health and Beauty

"It's for hair loss awareness".

Health and Beauty

"It's so thoughtful of your boss to send you a card Brian."

Health and Beauty

"No one is making fun of you. You're just being overly sensitive."

JOKE OF THE DAY

Just before the Ark set sail, Noah saw
his two sons fishing over the side.
'Go easy on the bait,' he said,
'Remember I've only got two worms.'

160

Higher Education

Higher Education

"He's really putting that media studies degree to good use."

163

Higher Education

"I've just realised something! - Thirty three years he's been at university!"

Higher Education

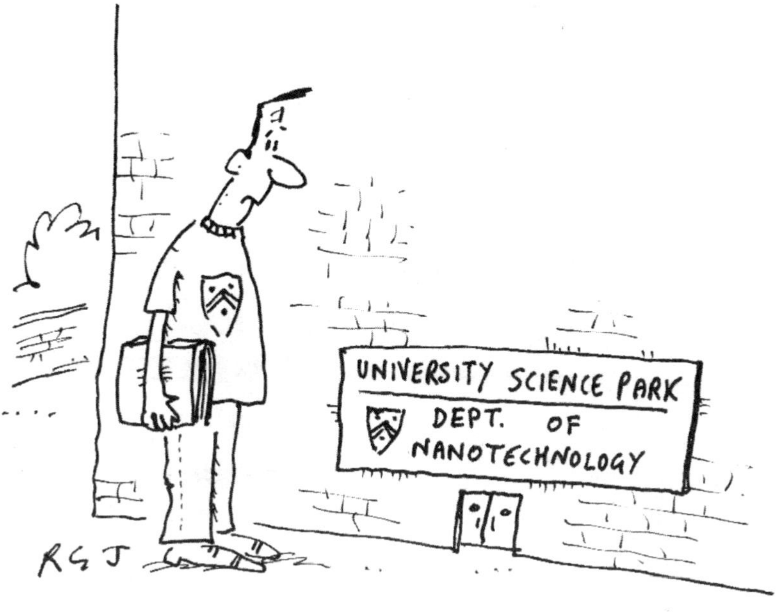
UNIVERSITY SCIENCE PARK
DEPT. OF
NANOTECHNOLOGY
RGJ

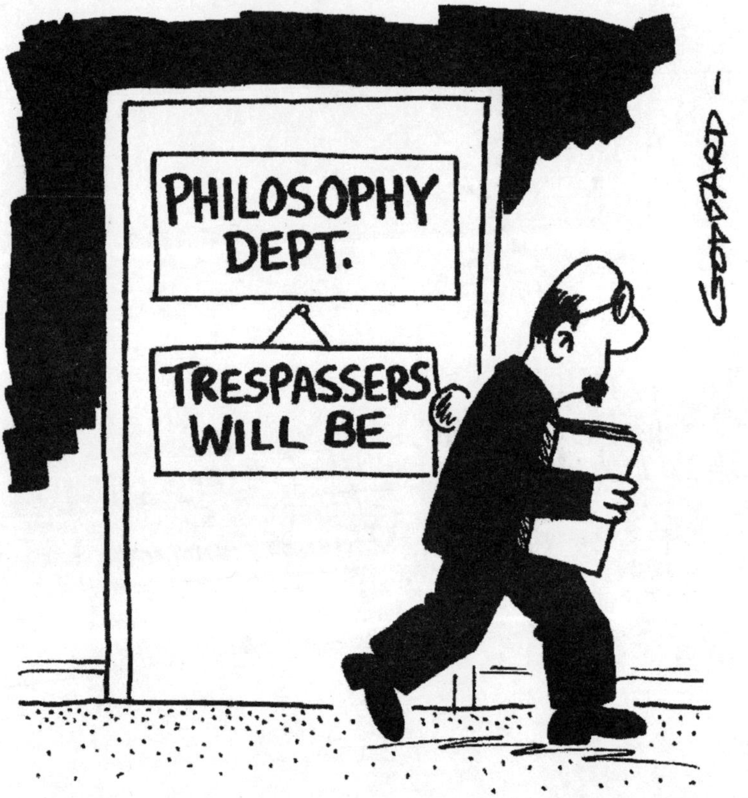
PHILOSOPHY DEPT.
TRESPASSERS WILL BE
GODDARD

Higher Education

"Mum, Dad, I've decided to go to University.
I want to party for five years before I start work."

167

Higher Education

"Today: The collective unconscious..."

Higher Education

"I'm sorry, we're looking for somebody with experience."

169

Higher Education

Higher Education

Halfway around the
learning curve, Bob let go.

THOUGHT
FOR THE DAY

Against boredom, even the gods struggle in vain.

NIETZSCHE

History

History

"Wow! - Is that the new Pipe-x 176 Z series mobile phone?"

History

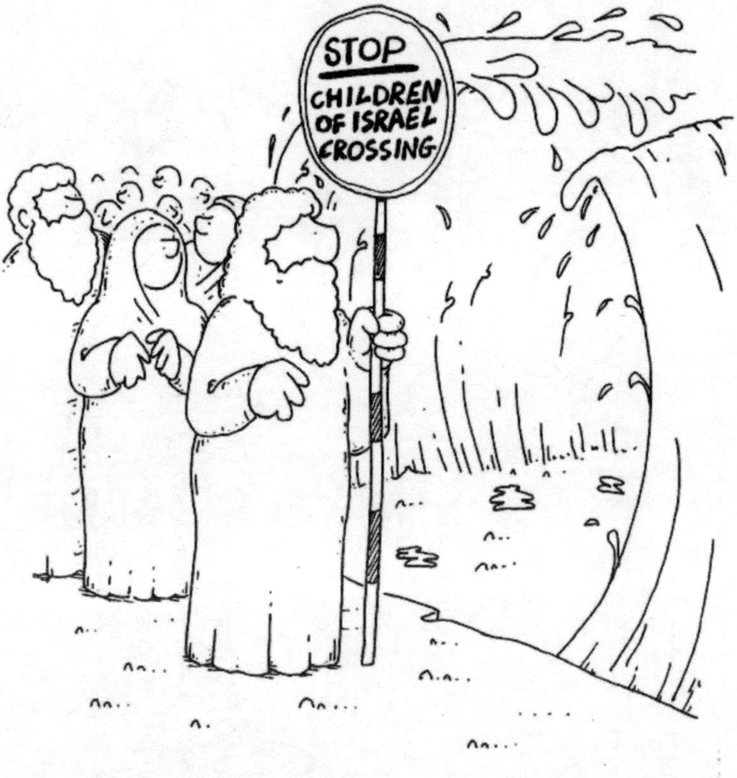
STOP
CHILDREN OF ISRAEL CROSSING

History

'Bay-owulf'

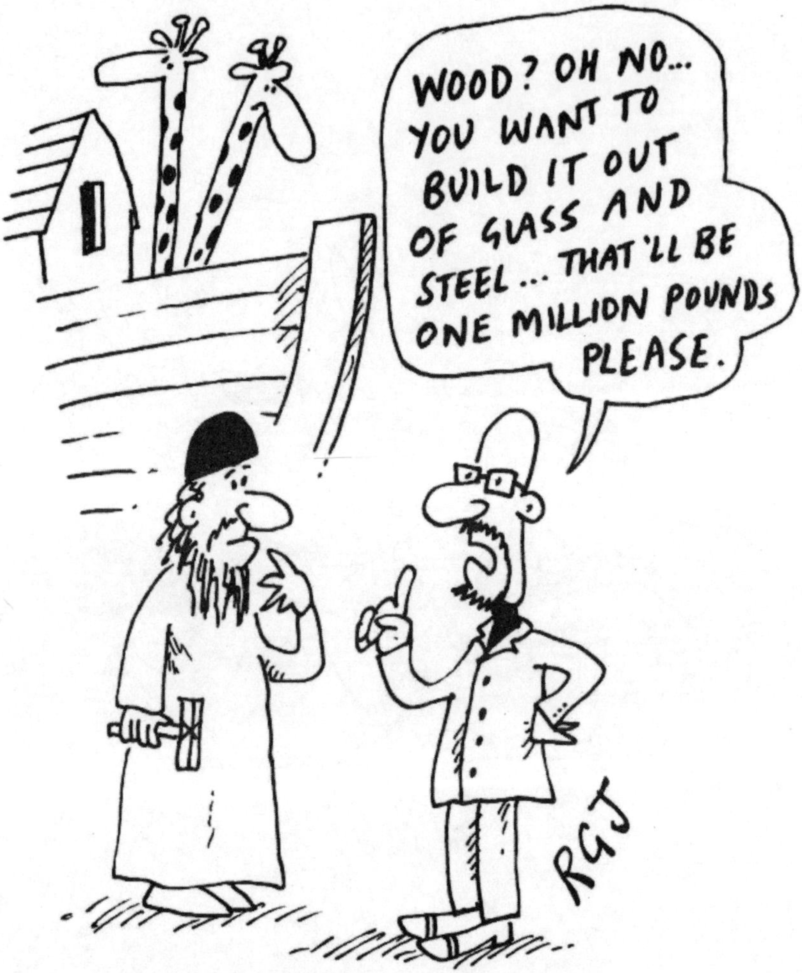
WOOD? OH NO... YOU WANT TO BUILD IT OUT OF GLASS AND STEEL... THAT'LL BE ONE MILLION POUNDS PLEASE.
RGJ
NOAH'S ARCHITECT

"It appears to be some sort of tax cut promise."

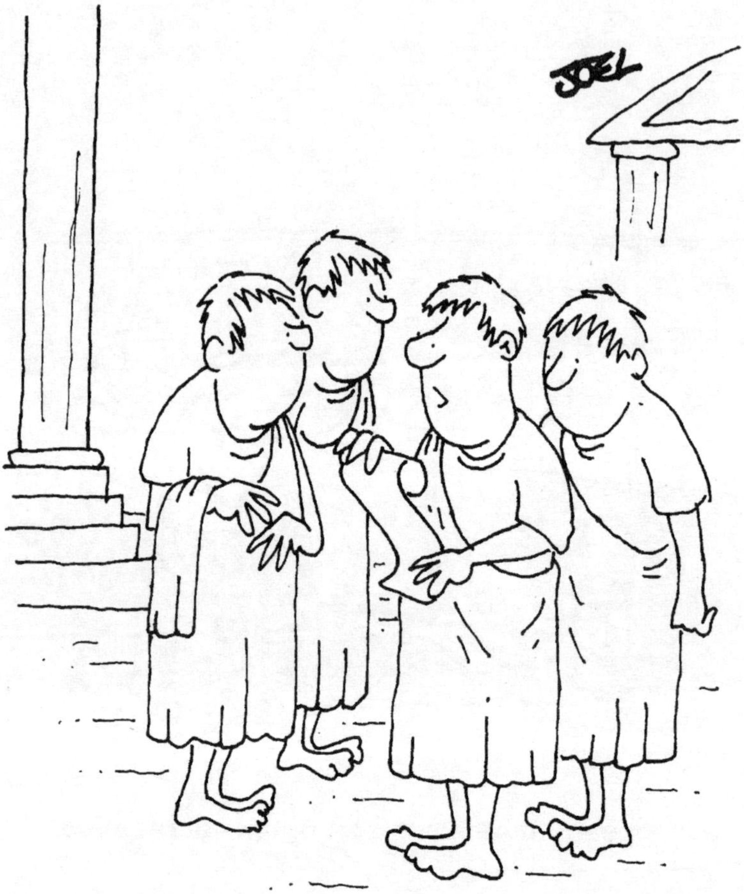
JOEL

"It's another toga party."

History

BUT DR JOHNSON, OF WAT YUSE WIL
THIS DICSHUNARY OF YOURS BE?

History

NEANDERTHAL MAN
RODNEY MICKLETHWAITE

RODNEYS FAMILY TREE WAS A LOT SHORTER THAN MOST

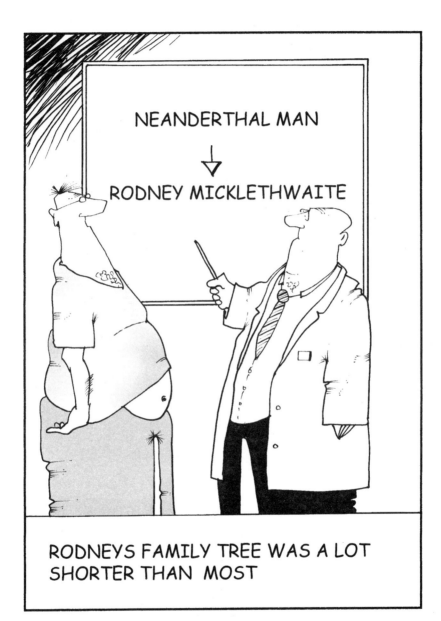

Home Improvement

Home Improvement

"Peter says all these decorating programmes have given
him a marvellous idea!"

Home Improvement

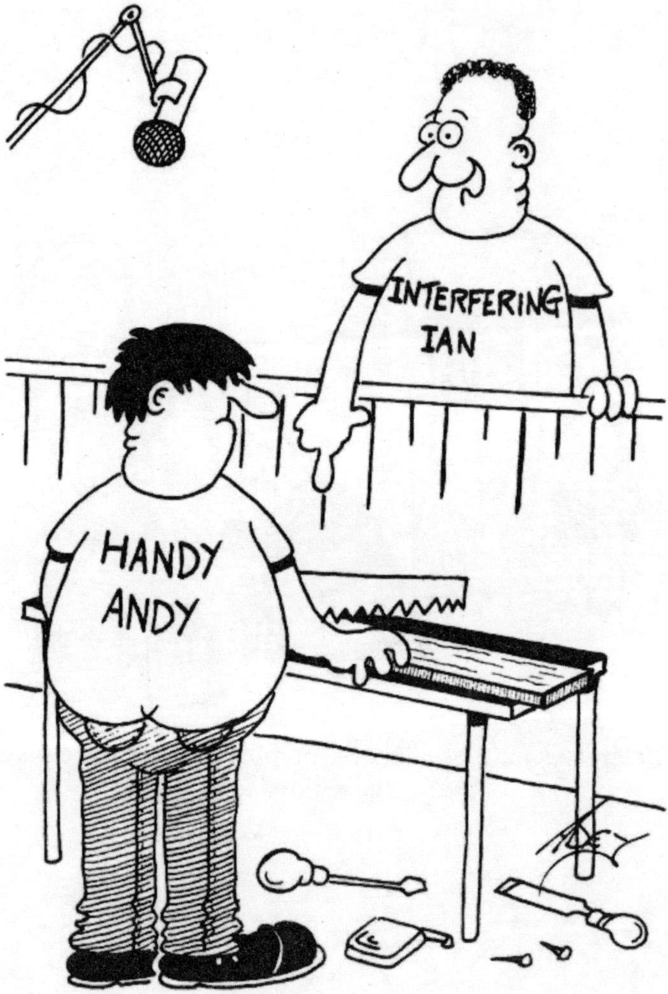
INTERFERING IAN
HANDY ANDY

Home Improvement

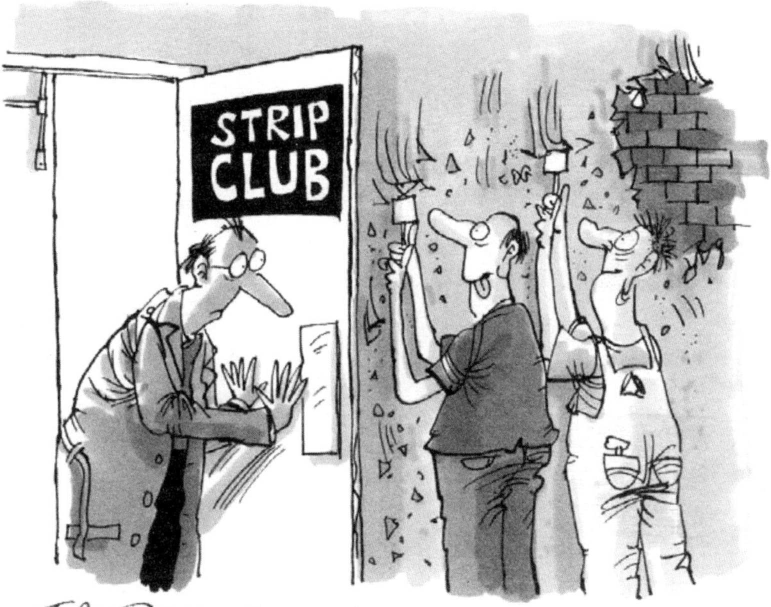
STRIP CLUB
IAN BAKER.

"Errr... could I see your qualifications again, Mr. Barker?"

Home Improvement

"Sorry we've run out of sandpaper but this does
a very similar job."

Home Improvement

Convenience, security and a whole lot of fun. Power windows for the home.

"No, I've changed my mind again,
it looked better over there."

Home Improvement

"He came to help me pick out a pattern that I won't just get tired of after 30 or 40 years."

Home Improvement

Home Improvement

'...BUT IF I LET THEM GO, WHAT HAPPENS NEXT TIME WE NEED WORK DONE ON THE HOUSE?!'

JOKE OF THE DAY

A Californian man has invented a robotic parking attendant. He's calling it the Silicon Valet.

THOUGHT
FOR THE DAY

Law of conservation of confusion: the total amount of confusion in this world remains constant. It just gets shifted around.

Law and Order

Law and Order

"Bit the wrong guy."

Law and Order

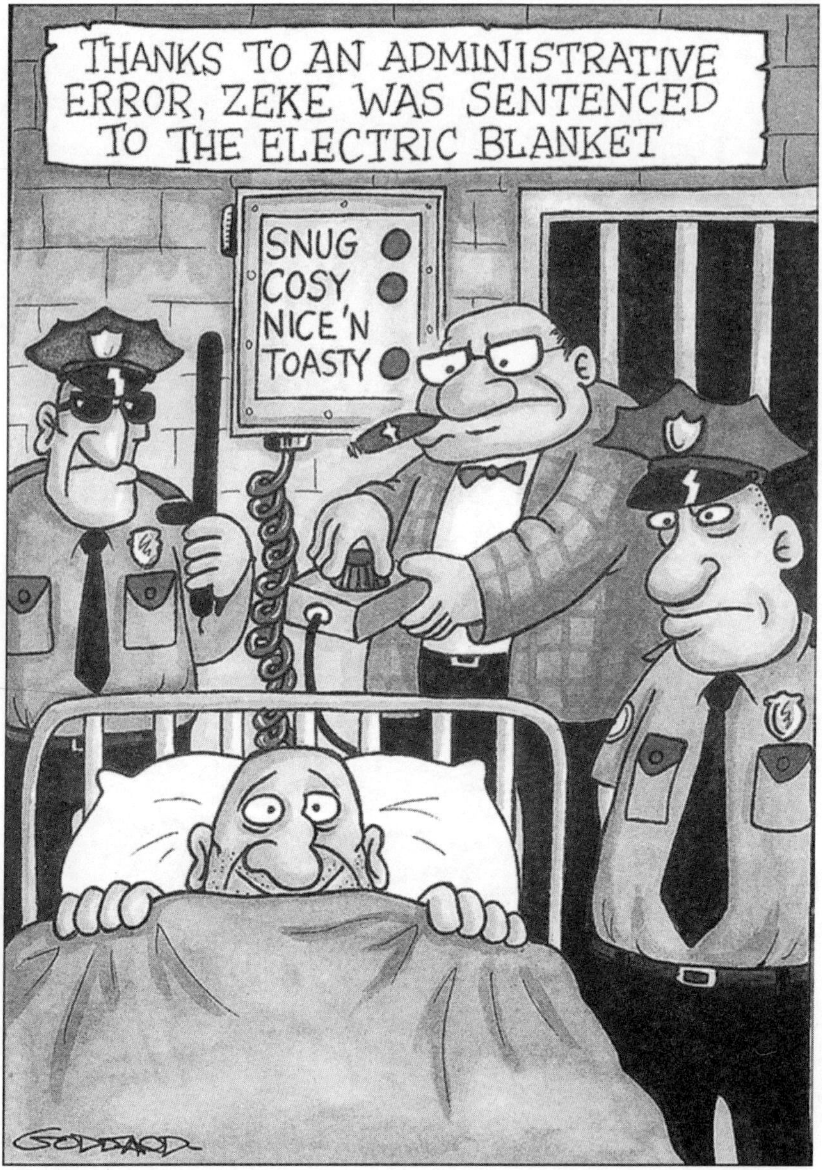
THANKS TO AN ADMINISTRATIVE ERROR, ZEKE WAS SENTENCED TO THE ELECTRIC BLANKET
SNUG
COSY
NICE 'N TOASTY
GODDARD

Law and Order

"OK, I'll read you your rights once more, but then it's lights out, no more talking 'til morning or your lawyers are present."

INSULT

OF THE DAY

He is the same old sausage, fizzing and sputtering in his own grease.

HENRY JAMES

Law and Order

"Oooh - a Valentines card. I wonder who it's from?"

Law and Order

"Your nails look much better. But that wasn't why I slipped you the file."

"Now that's what I call organised crime."

"Tails it is. We find the defendant guilty."

Law and Order

'COULD YOU STEAL THAT ONE, IT'S ON
A DOUBLE YELLOW LINE'

Law and Order

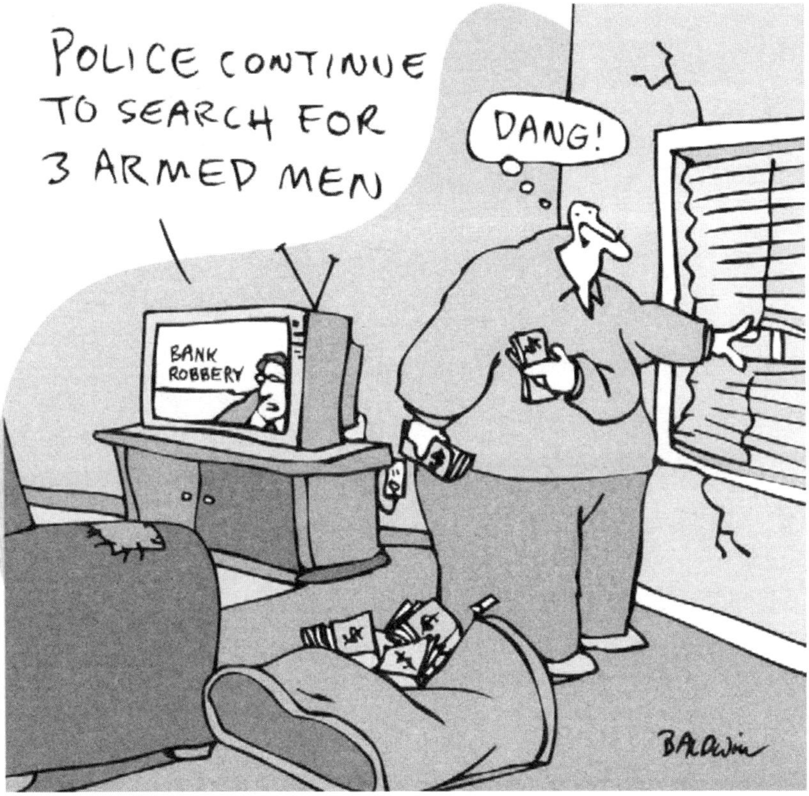

POLICE CONTINUE TO SEARCH FOR 3 ARMED MEN
DANG!
BANK ROBBERY
BALDWIN

Law and Order

HE'S UPSET BECAUSE THE FRAUDSTERS WHO
STOLE HIS IDENTITY GAVE IT BACK...

Law and Order

'DON'T STOP THAT THIEF!
IT'LL BE TOO MUCH PAPERWORK'

Law and Order

"I've heard some lame excuses in my time, but 'I'm only 7' takes the cake."

INSULT

OF THE DAY

She is such a bad cook that she uses the smoke alarm as a timer.

JOKE OF THE DAY

A man walked into a pub and saw a gorilla serving behind the bar.

'What's the matter?' said the gorilla, realizing he was being stared at. 'Have you never seen a gorilla serving drinks before?'

'It's not that,' said the man. 'I just never thought the giraffe would sell this place.'

Media

"Ok, now let's get one of you demanding your privacy."

Media

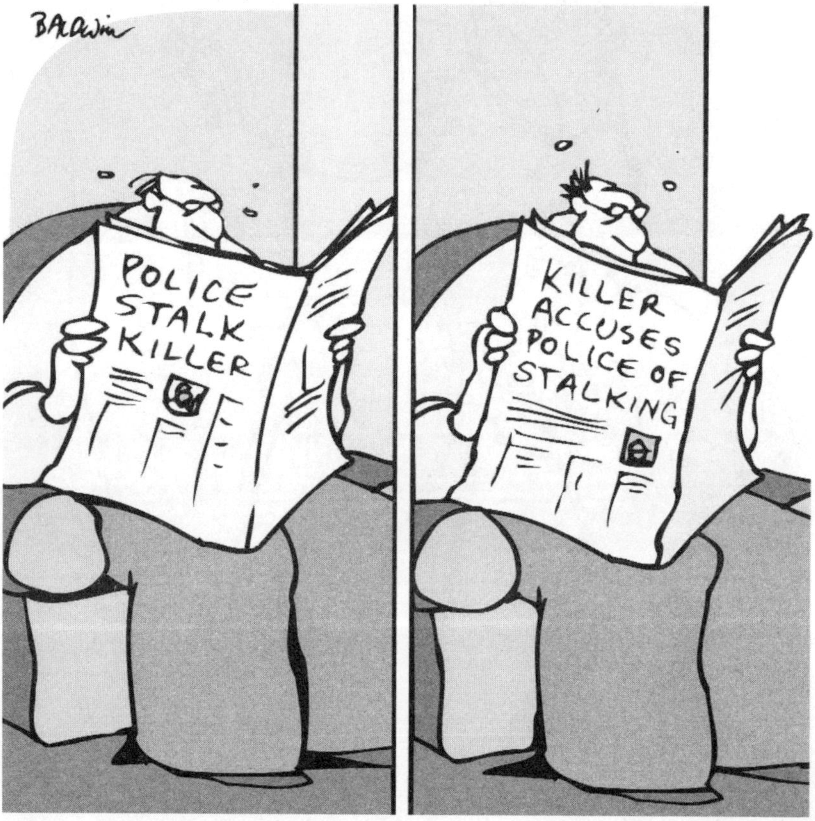
BALDWIN
POLICE STALK KILLER
KILLER ACCUSES POLICE OF STALKING

Media

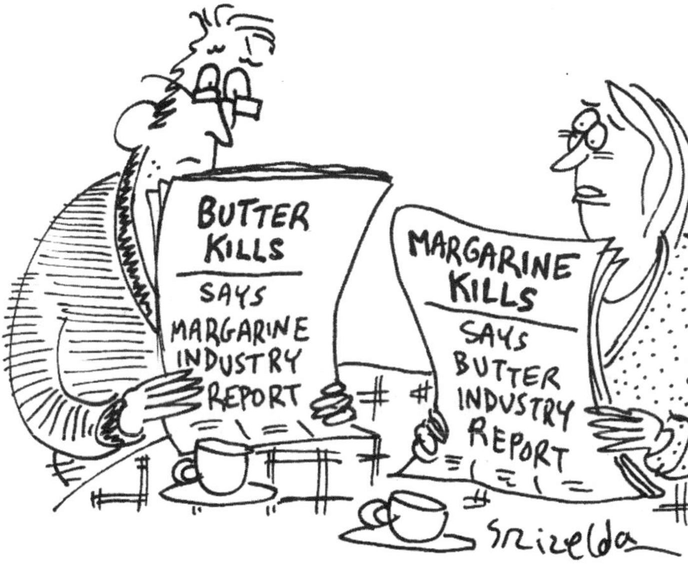
BUTTER KILLS
SAYS MARGARINE INDUSTRY REPORT
MARGARINE KILLS
SAYS BUTTER INDUSTRY REPORT
Grizelda

IT'S A BLOOD CURDLING NOVEL ABOUT THE BRUTAL MURDER OF A PUBLISHER WHO REJECTED A BOOK ABOUT THE BRUTAL MURDER OF A PUBLISHER...

Media

"It's that idiot reporter again from the National Enquirer."

THE THERAPY **DID** HELP YOUR HUSBAND FIND HIS INNER CHILD...UNFORTUNATELY HIS INNER CHILD IS CALLED DWAYNE.

THOUGHT
FOR THE DAY

Collaboration is essential: it allows you to blame someone else.

INSULT

OF THE DAY

She has the sort of charm that rubs off with tissues and cold cream.

224

Military and War

Military and War

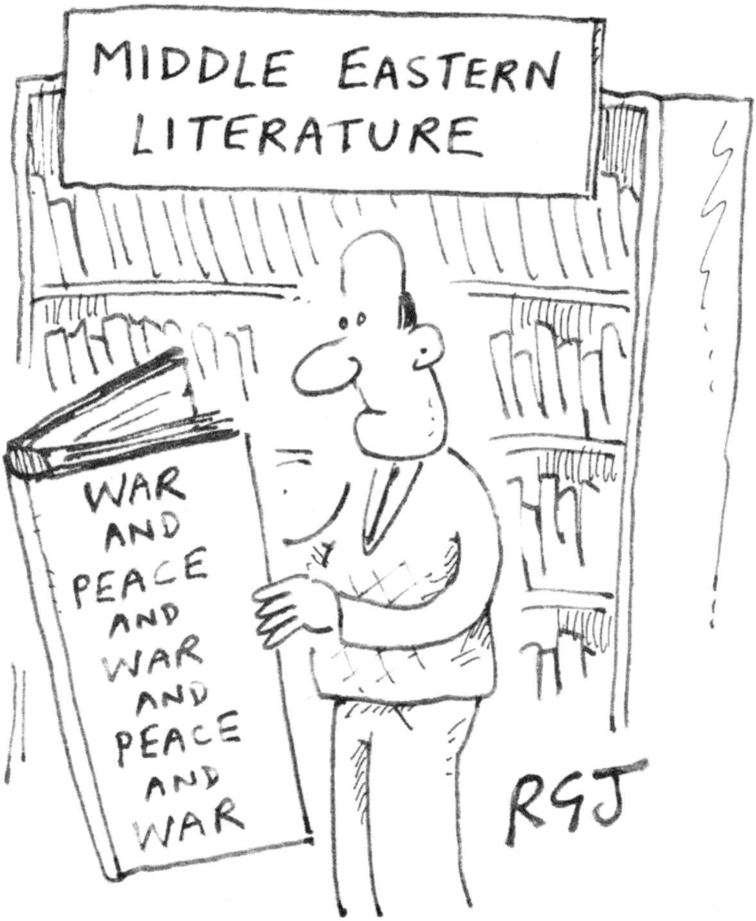
MIDDLE EASTERN
LITERATURE
WAR
AND
PEACE
AND
WAR
AND
PEACE
AND
WAR
RGJ

Military and War

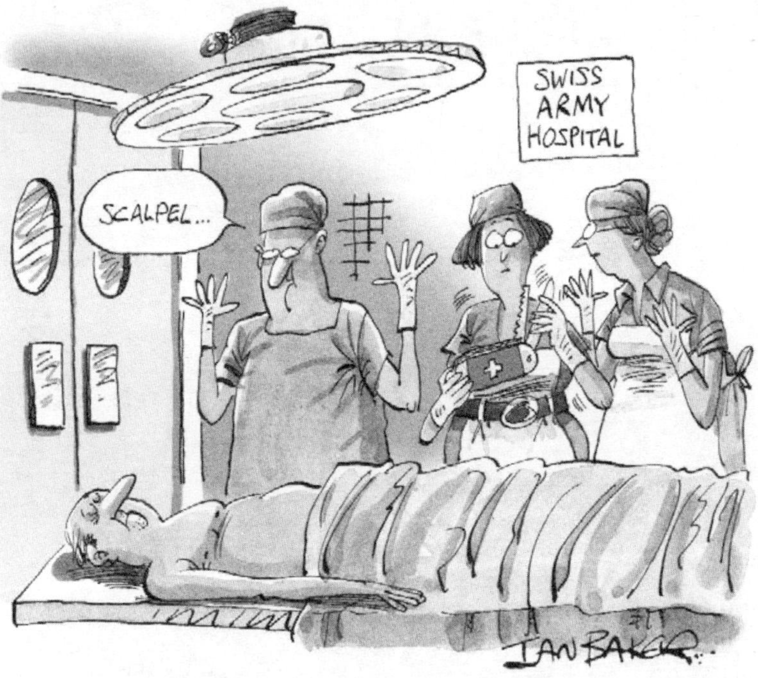
SWISS ARMY HOSPITAL
SCALPEL...
IAN BAKER

Military and War

WAR PROTESTER

"Oh no! Not this again ... "

"Possible security breach, sir. It's the smart bombs. They know too much."

Military and War

TROOP THERAPY

"Nice going. That was one of our guys, just trying to clean out the gutters."

THE BIN WAS KICKED OVER AT 3am
THERE IS NO EVIDENCE OF TERRORIST
INVOLVEMENT, JOHN STOKES BBC NEWS

JOKE OF THE DAY

A Zen Master walked up to a hot-dog seller and said: 'Make me one with everything.'

Modern Technology

Modern Technology

FOR SAFETY REASONS WE RECOMMEND
THAT YOU USE TRADITIONAL RINGING
TONES WHEN PROGRAMMING YOUR PHONE

237

Modern Technology

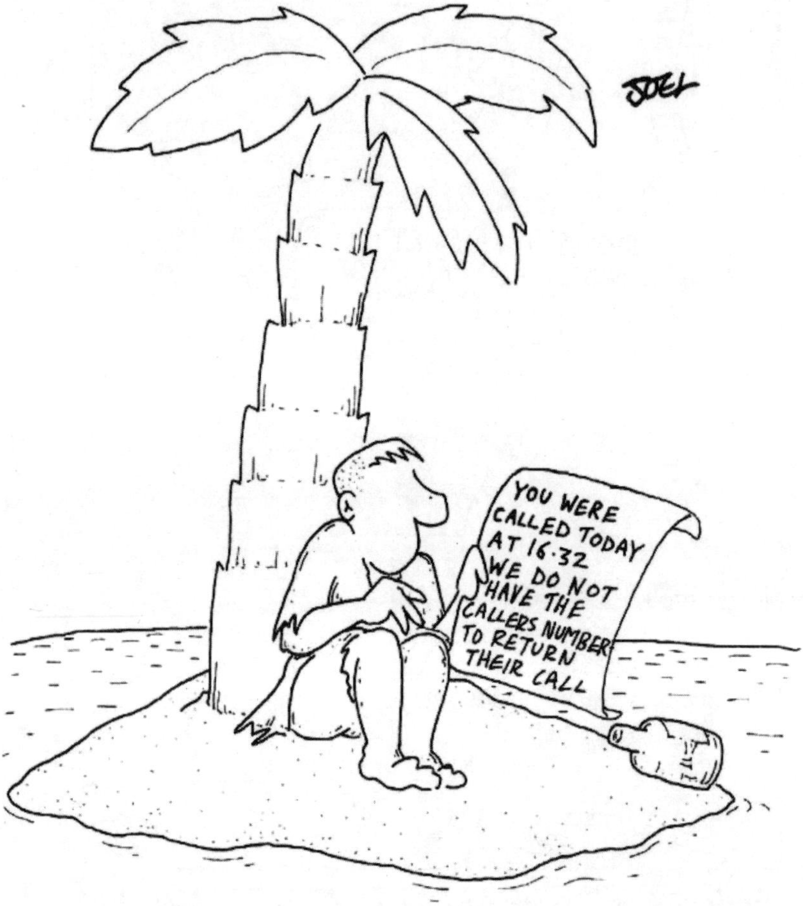
JOEL
YOU WERE CALLED TODAY AT 16.32 WE DO NOT HAVE THE CALLERS NUMBER TO RETURN THEIR CALL

Modern Technology

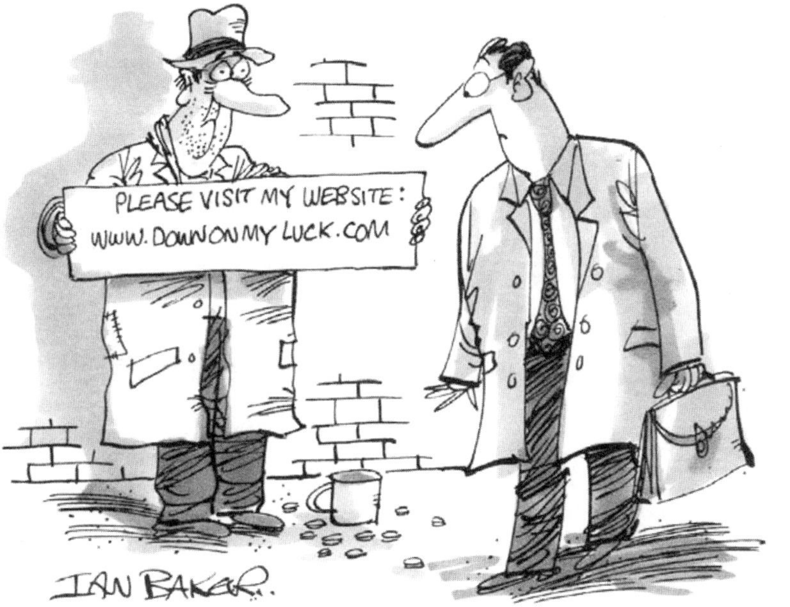
PLEASE VISIT MY WEBSITE:
WWW.DOWNONMYLUCK.COM
IAN BAKER.

"Unfinished business used to mean going back as a ghost. Now, thanks to the Web, you can work from here."

Modern Technology

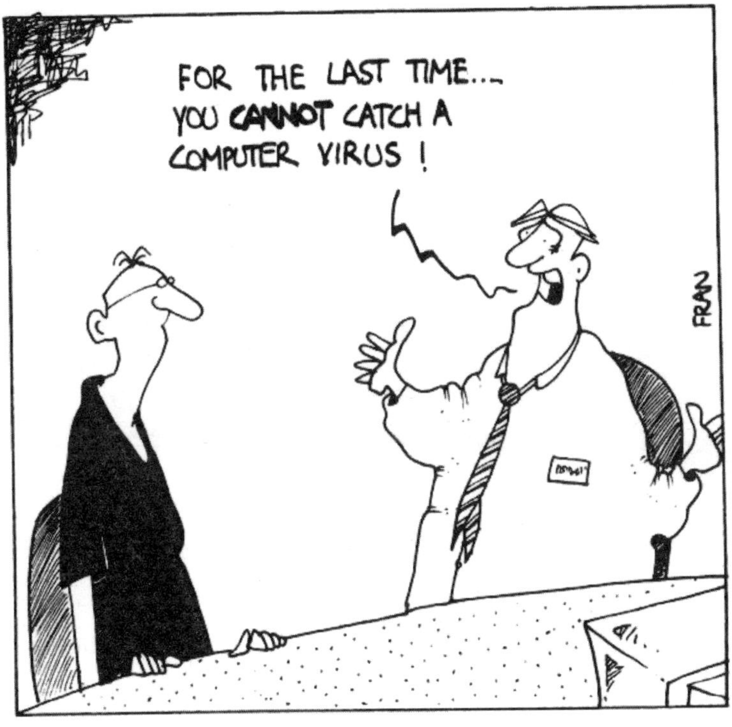
FOR THE LAST TIME...
YOU CANNOT CATCH A
COMPUTER VIRUS !
FRAN

Modern Technology

Some just ain't cut out for wind farmin'.

Modern Technology

MONICA WAS CONCERNED THAT
COLIN WAS OVER-DEPENDANT UPON
HIS MOBILE PHONE

243

THOUGHT
FOR THE DAY

I live in fear of not being misunderstood.

OSCAR WILDE

INSULT
OF THE DAY

I have nothing but
confidence in you.
And very little of that.

GROUCHO MARX

JOKE OF THE DAY

A man called over to his neighbour one morning: 'Did you hear me thumping on the wall last night?'

'Oh, don't worry about it! We were making a fair bit of noise ourselves.'

Money

Money

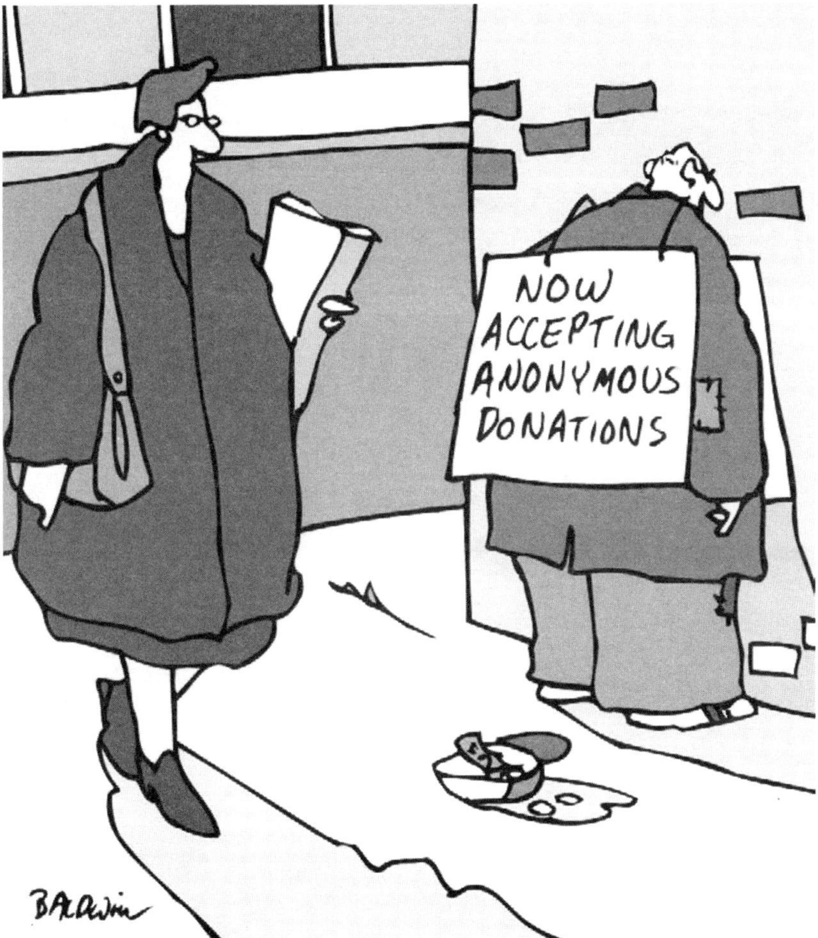
NOW ACCEPTING ANONYMOUS DONATIONS
BALDWIN

Money

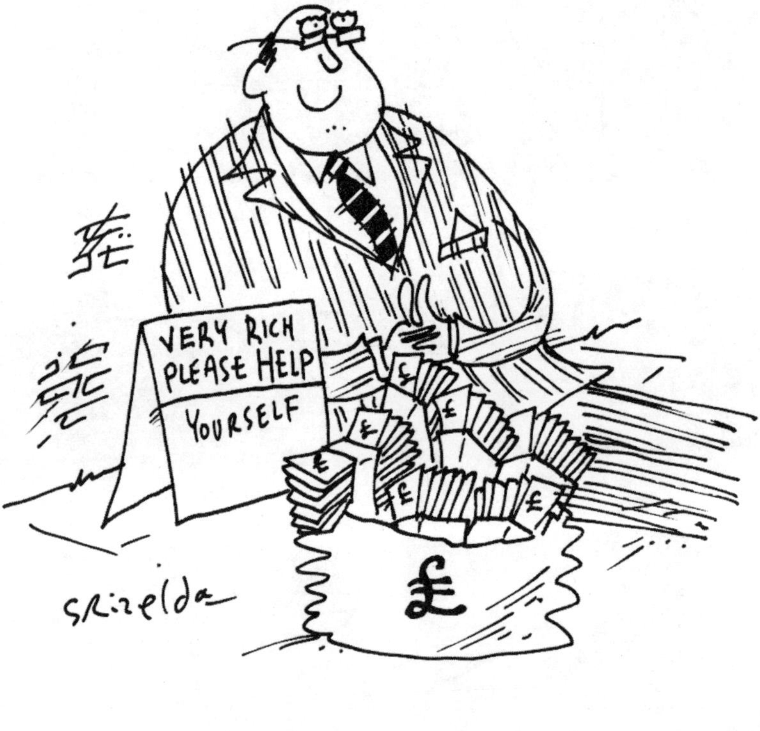
VERY RICH
PLEASE HELP
YOURSELF
£

Money

FRIDGE MAGNATE

"Damn! Telephone banking."

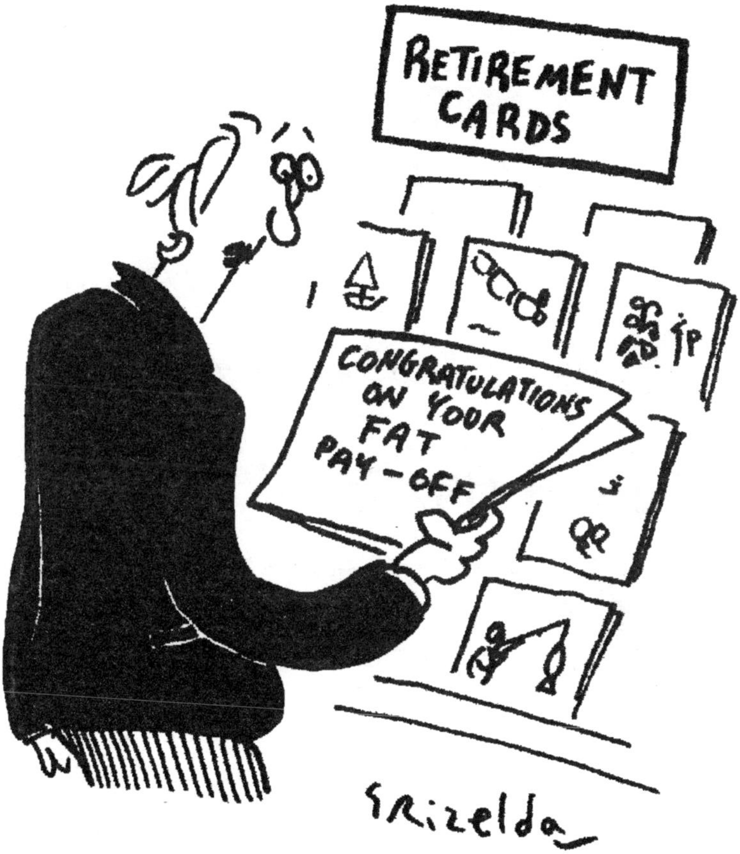
RETIREMENT CARDS
CONGRATULATIONS ON YOUR FAT PAY-OFF
GRizelda

Money

"Can I have a receipt?"

"I like to keep a few pictures of my
loved ones on my desk."

THOUGHT
FOR THE DAY

If you can't make yourself feel better, the least you can do is make someone else feel worse.

Movies

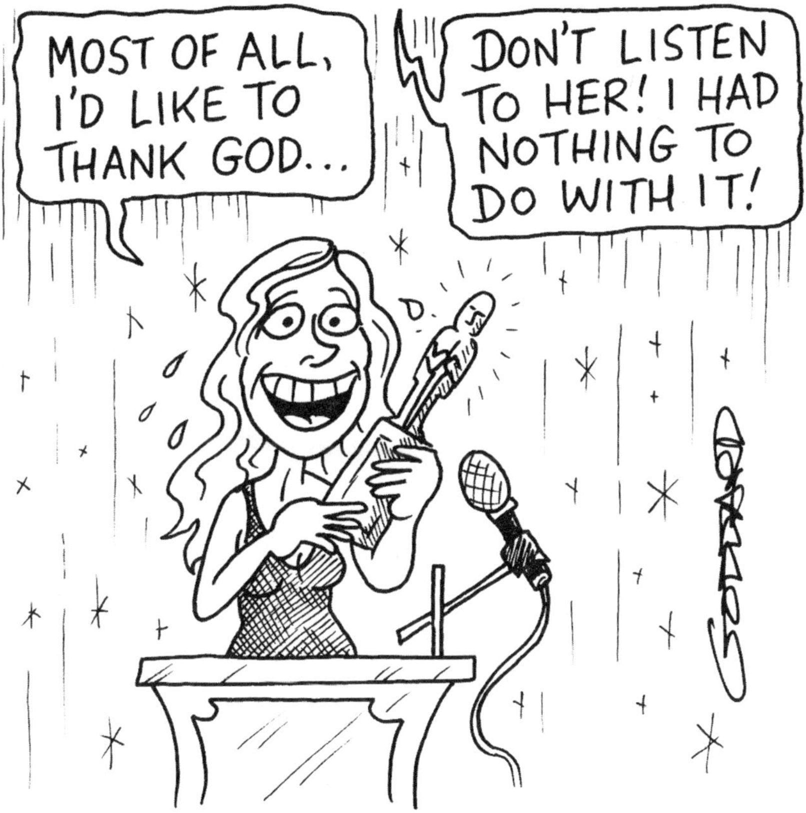
MOST OF ALL, I'D LIKE TO THANK GOD...
DON'T LISTEN TO HER! I HAD NOTHING TO DO WITH IT!

"We're going to have to cancel the light sabre duel, Darth–
unless you've got two AA batteries you could lend me."

Movies

"...And the best product placement in a film award goes to.........."

261

'...we can only pay you $20 million for your next film — Video piracy is killing the film industry'

Movies

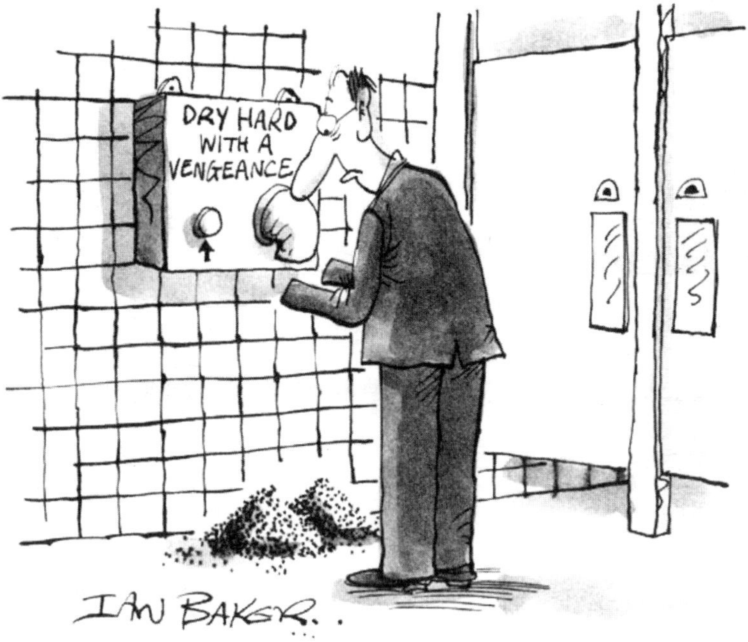
DRY HARD
WITH A
VENGEANCE
IAN BAKER

Movies

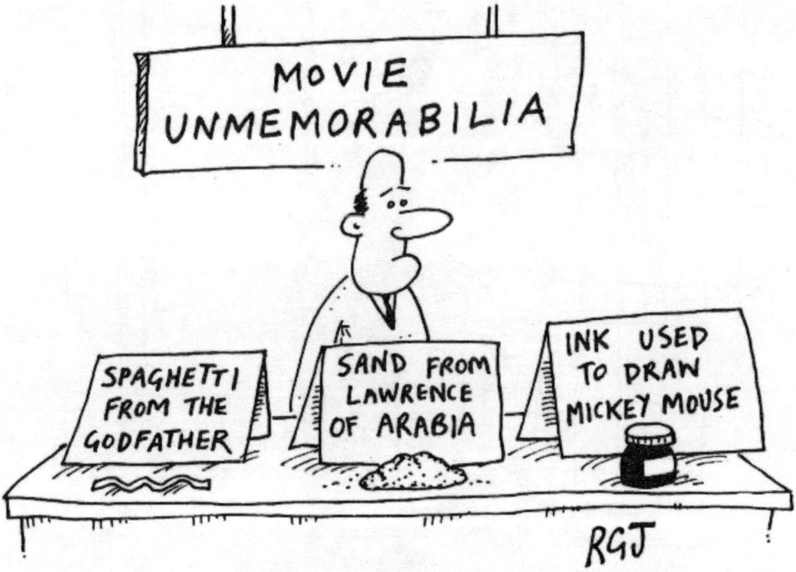
MOVIE UNMEMORABILIA
SPAGHETTI FROM THE GODFATHER
SAND FROM LAWRENCE OF ARABIA
INK USED TO DRAW MICKEY MOUSE
RGJ

Winner of the Worst Slogan Contest.

THE UNUSUAL SUSPECTS

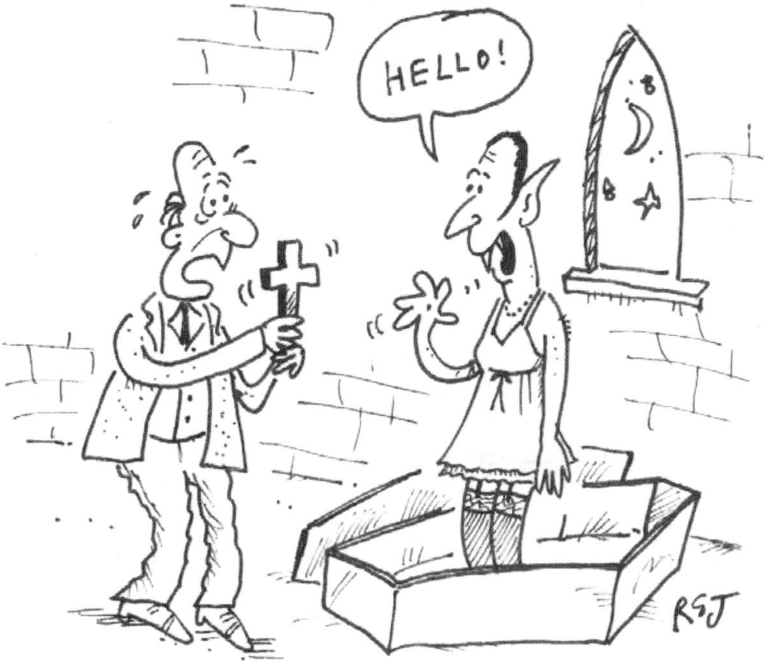
HELLO!
RSJ

"Oh, no! Count Dragula!"

INSULT
OF THE DAY

You take the lies out of him and he'll shrink to the size of your hat; you take the malice out of him, and he'll disappear.

MARK TWAIN

Music

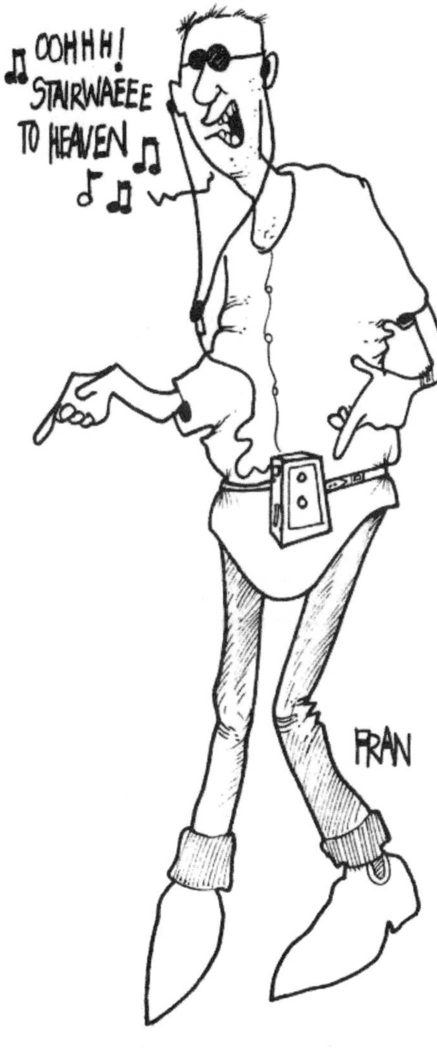
OOHHH!
STAIRWAEEE
TO HEAVEN
FRAN

SONY DORKMAN

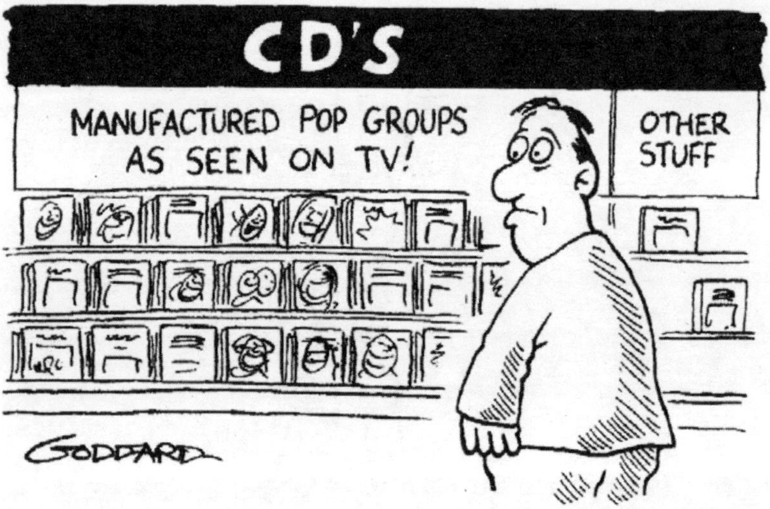
CD'S
MANUFACTURED POP GROUPS AS SEEN ON TV!
OTHER STUFF
GODDARD

Music

"Used to sing the blues. Started popping Prozac and lost everything."

"Hurry Doctor!
This man has Saturday Night Fever!"

Music

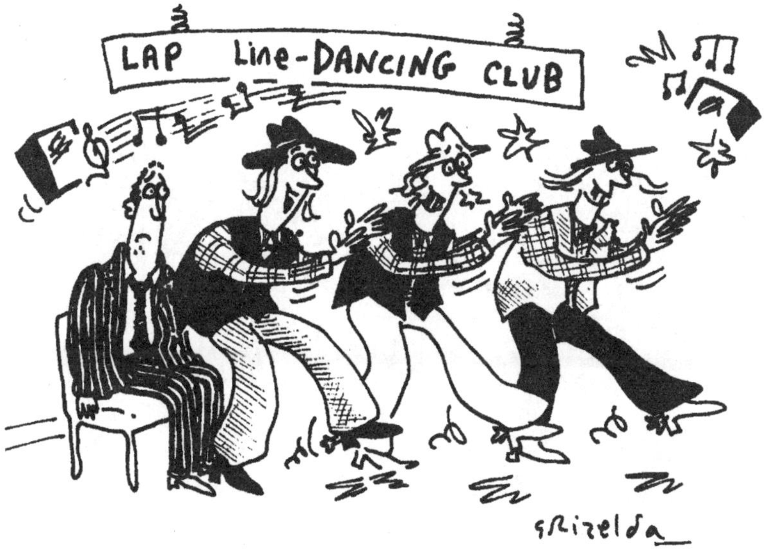
LAP Line-DANCING CLUB
GRizelda

"Those '70s flashbacks scare the Bee-Gees-us out of me."

NEXT TIME, DON'T SUCK SO HARD!
FRAN
BAGPIPE TRAINING SCHOOL

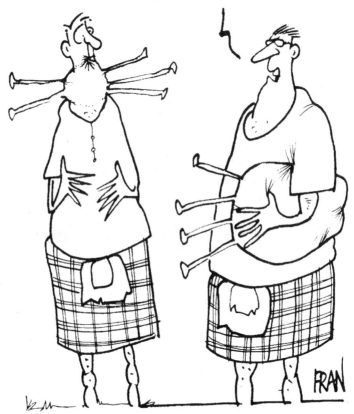

JOKE OF THE DAY

Why did the escaped convict saw the
legs off his bed?
    He wanted to lie low.

THOUGHT
FOR THE DAY

The best time to do
nothing is whenever and
as often as you can.

INSULT

OF THE DAY

If you see two people talking and one looks bored, he's the other one.

Politics

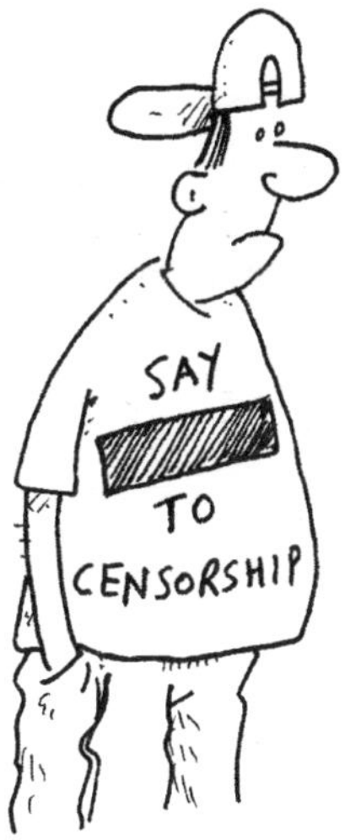
SAY
[redacted]
TO
CENSORSHIP

"Now can we have it as a sound bite ?"

283

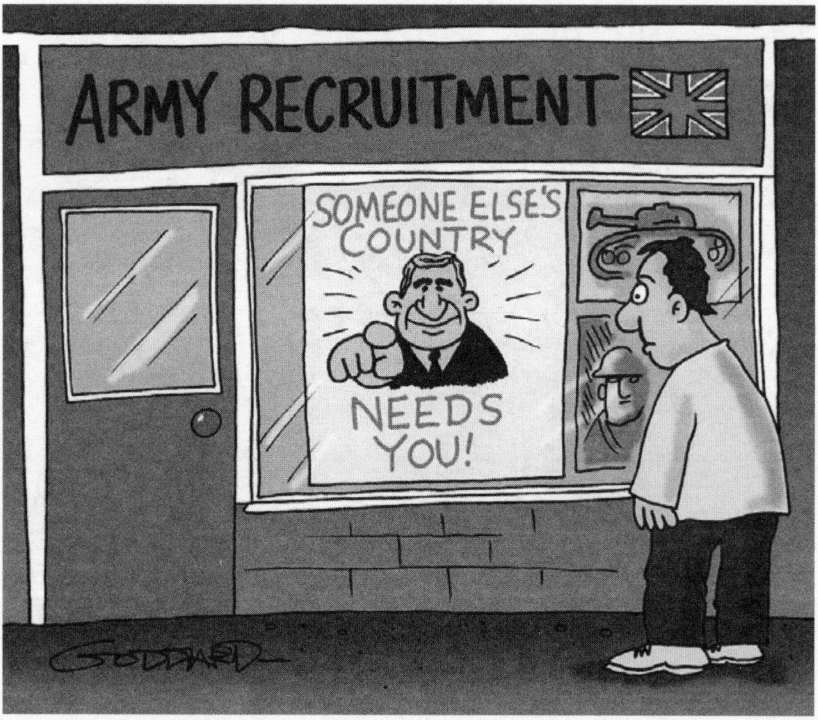
ARMY RECRUITMENT
SOMEONE ELSE'S COUNTRY
NEEDS YOU!

Politics

"What are your comments on press intrusion "

285

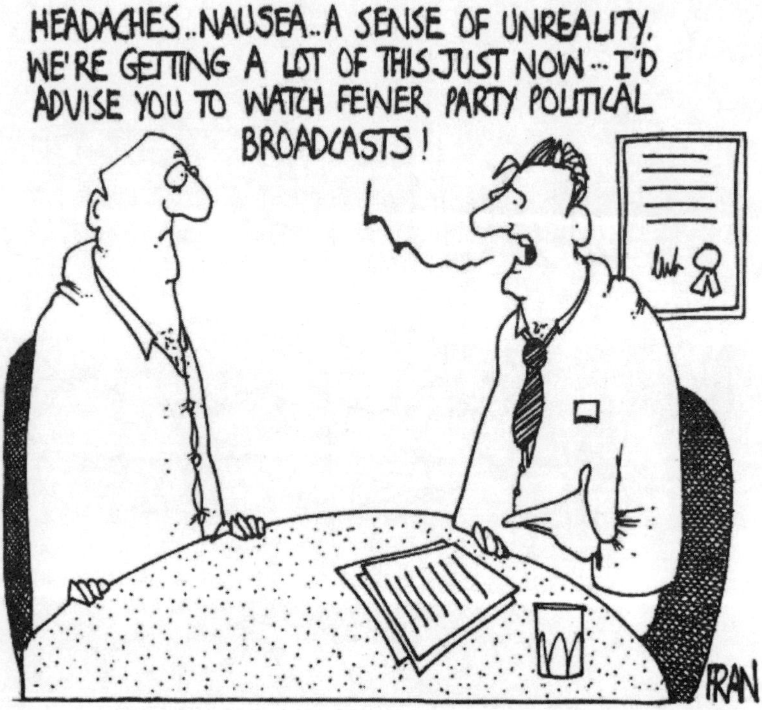
HEADACHES..NAUSEA..A SENSE OF UNREALITY.
WE'RE GETTING A LOT OF THIS JUST NOW...I'D
ADVISE YOU TO WATCH FEWER PARTY POLITICAL
BROADCASTS!
FRAN

Politics

What they'd say if they really wanted the women's vote.

Politics

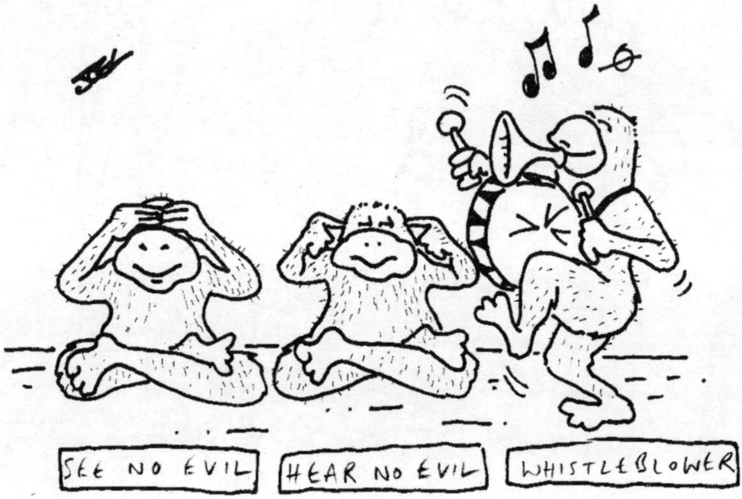

SEE NO EVIL
HEAR NO EVIL
WHISTLEBLOWER

"'Establish political equilibrium through balanced representation' wouldn't fit."

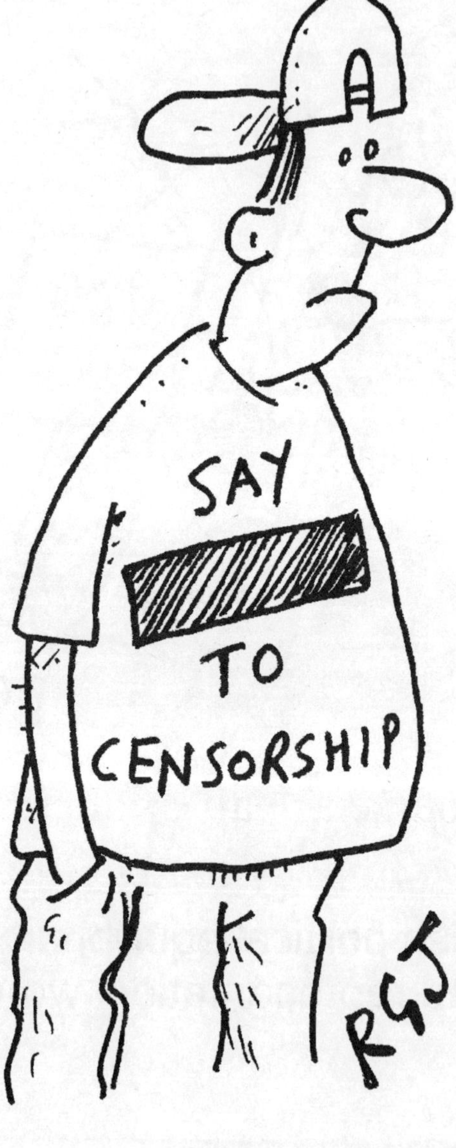
SAY
TO
CENSORSHIP
RGJ

"Of course as part of our ethical foreign policy the 20 kiloton population fragmentation bomb is only available to respectable governments."

INSULT
OF THE DAY

Some cause happiness
wherever they go; others
whenever they go.

Relationships

"Smirking or Non-Smirking ?"

Relationships

"What do you mean? Let's get undressed and make love? I am undressed."

Relationships

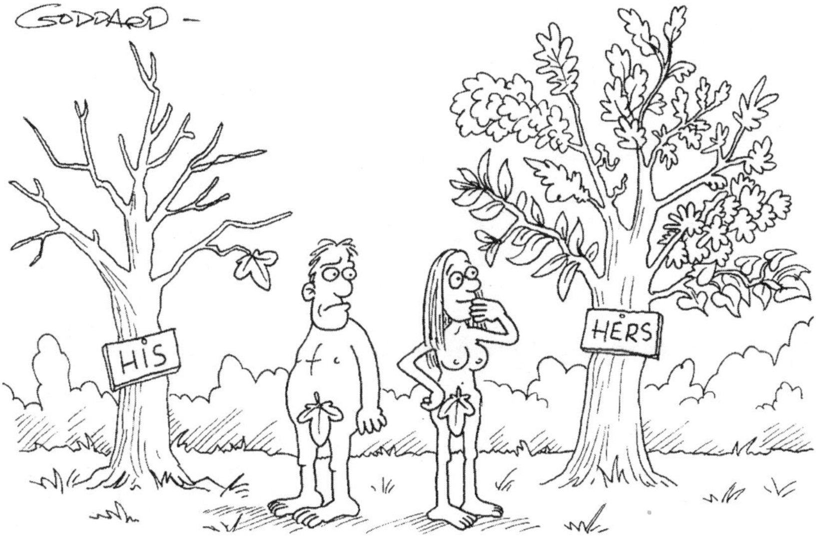
GODDARD -
HIS
HERS

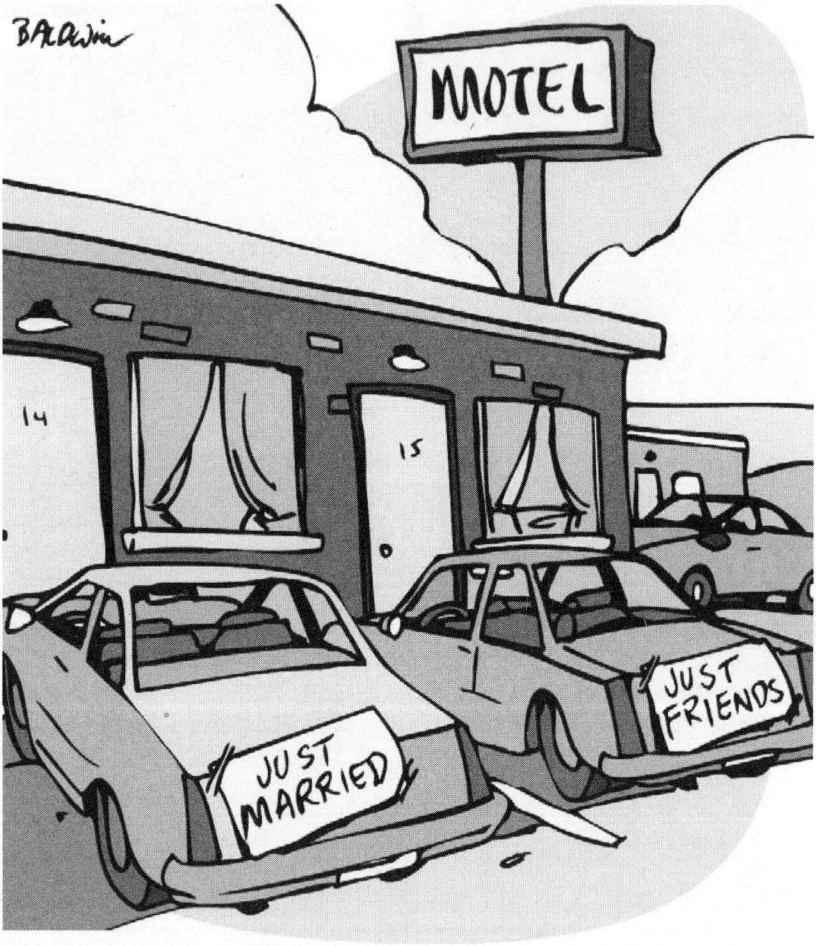
BALDWIN
MOTEL
14
15
JUST MARRIED
JUST FRIENDS

Relationships

"If we weren't married this would be romantic."

"The phone number is her idea. I think she wants to split up."

Relationships

"Ha-ha - two can play at your game. You've thrown all my clothes out, so I've come back and thrown all yours out!"

Relationships

STILL MARRIED

Relationships

She left him to go find herself.
It only took 20 minutes, which was sort
of embarrassing, so she decided to
hang out at the mall for a while.

"I want to divorce my husband he's having
an affair next week!"

Relationships

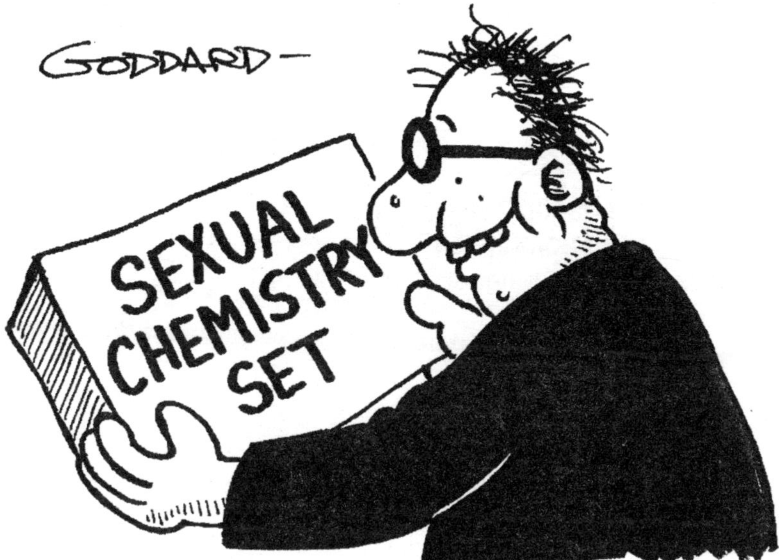
GODDARD
SEXUAL
CHEMISTRY
SET

JOKE OF THE DAY

Did you hear about the psychic dwarf who escaped from prison?

 The newspaper headline read: 'Small Medium at Large.'

THOUGHT
FOR THE DAY

Never underestimate the
power of human stupidity.

INSULT

OF THE DAY

He has all the virtues I dislike and none of the vices I admire.

Winston Churchill

School

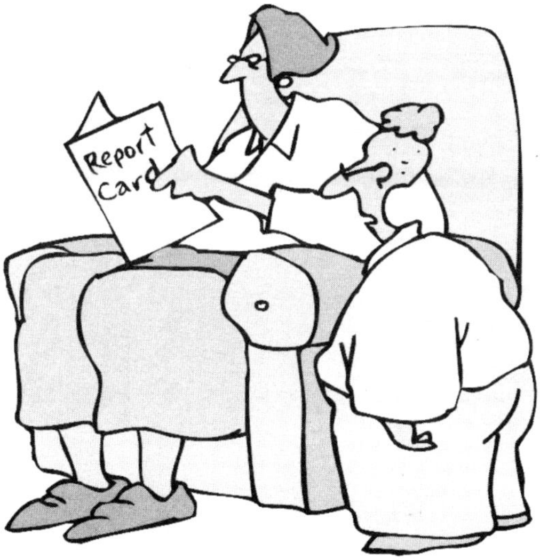
Report
Card

School

"Perhaps I possess the kind of wisdom that only comes with age."

School

BEFORE WE DO THE REGISTER..CAN ANY OF YOU
TEACH ENGLISH?

School

"I'd appreciate it if you'd wait until school to do that. We've worked long and hard to bring you state-of-the-art home theater."

School

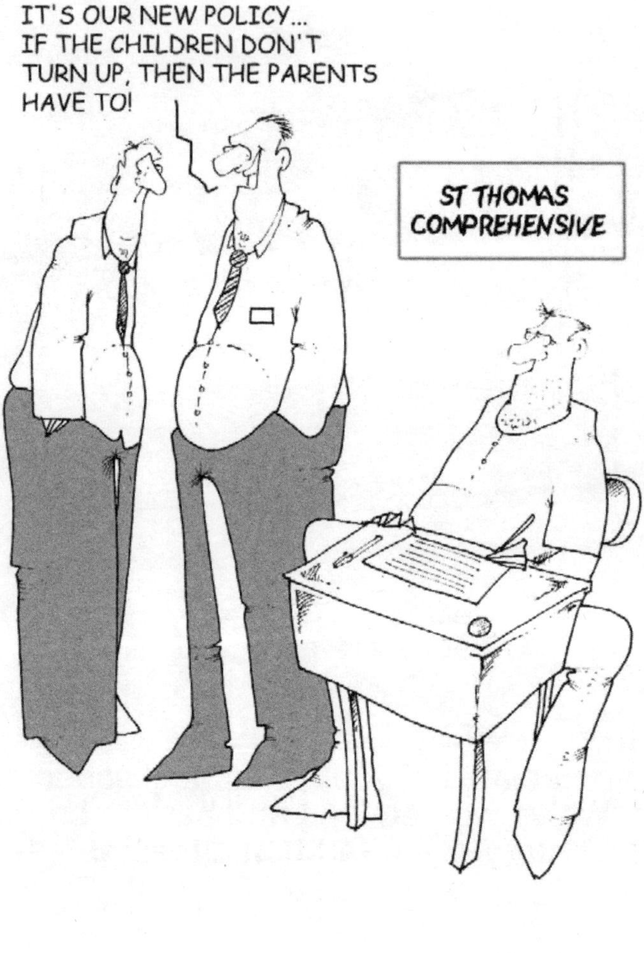
IT'S OUR NEW POLICY...
IF THE CHILDREN DON'T
TURN UP, THEN THE PARENTS
HAVE TO!
ST THOMAS
COMPREHENSIVE

"May I remind you that my core worth as a human being remains constant, and isn't tied to external validation."

"Very impressive. Leave it with me.
Mommy will get back to you by the
end of the week."

THOUGHT
FOR THE DAY

It's a dangerous dog that doesn't bark.

INSULT

OF THE DAY

I regard you with an indifference bordering on aversion.

ROBERT LOUIS STEVENSON

Science

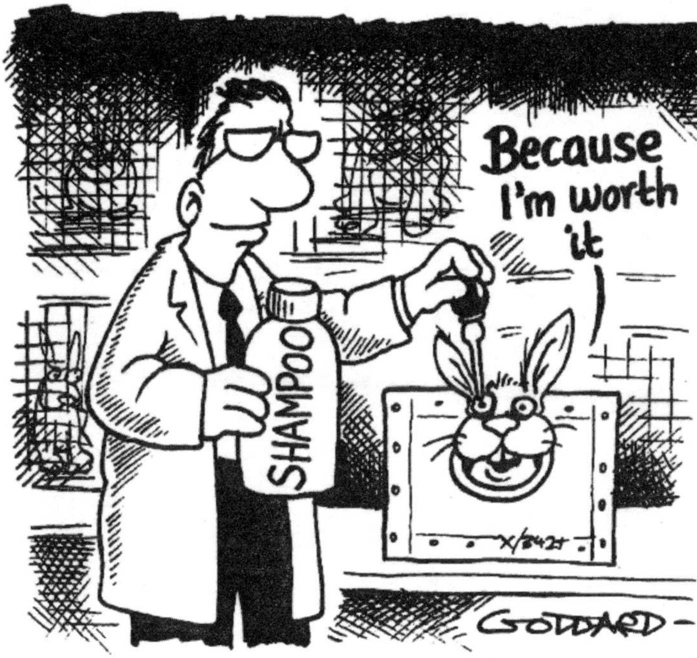
Because I'm worth it
SHAMPOO
GODDARD

Science

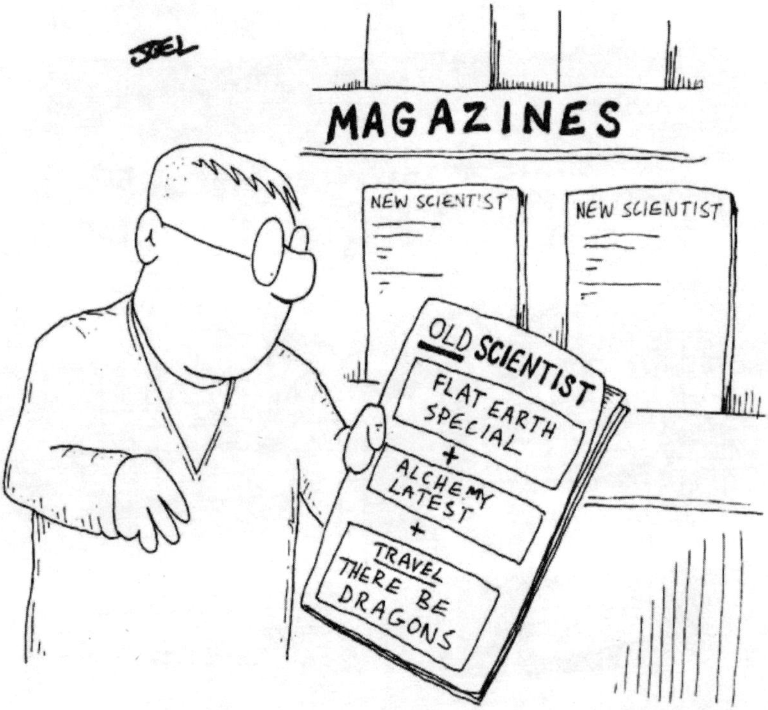
JOEL
MAGAZINES
NEW SCIENTIST
NEW SCIENTIST
OLD SCIENTIST
FLAT EARTH SPECIAL
+
ALCHEMY LATEST
+
TRAVEL
THERE BE DRAGONS

Science

'...and the award for best new-comer goes to..."

Science

Scientific Research Centre practical jokes

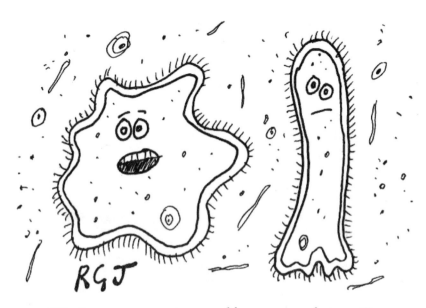

"My parents split up when I
was very young."

"Our scientists say it would be a public health hazard, but market research shows it would sell like hot cakes - what do you think?"

Science

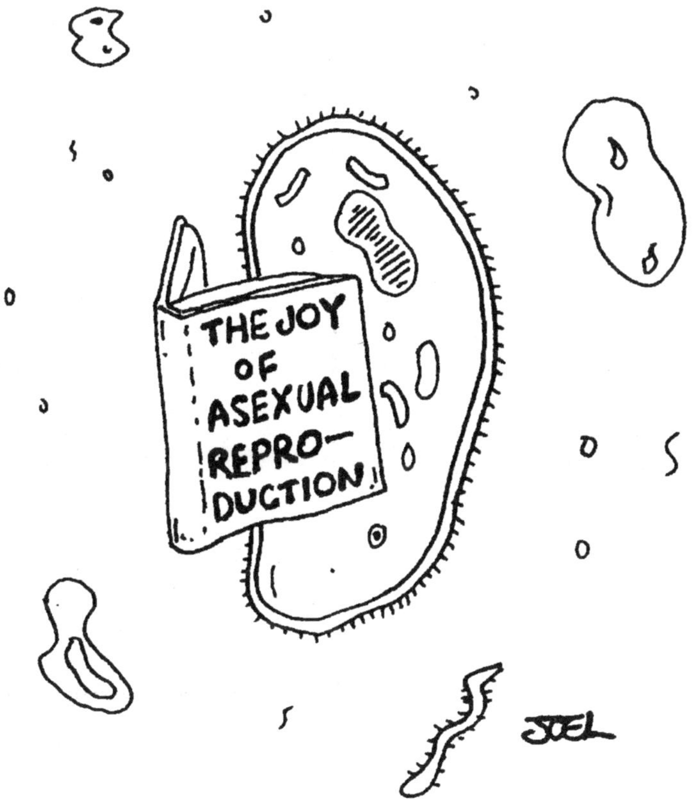
THE JOY
OF
ASEXUAL
REPRO-
DUCTION
JOEL

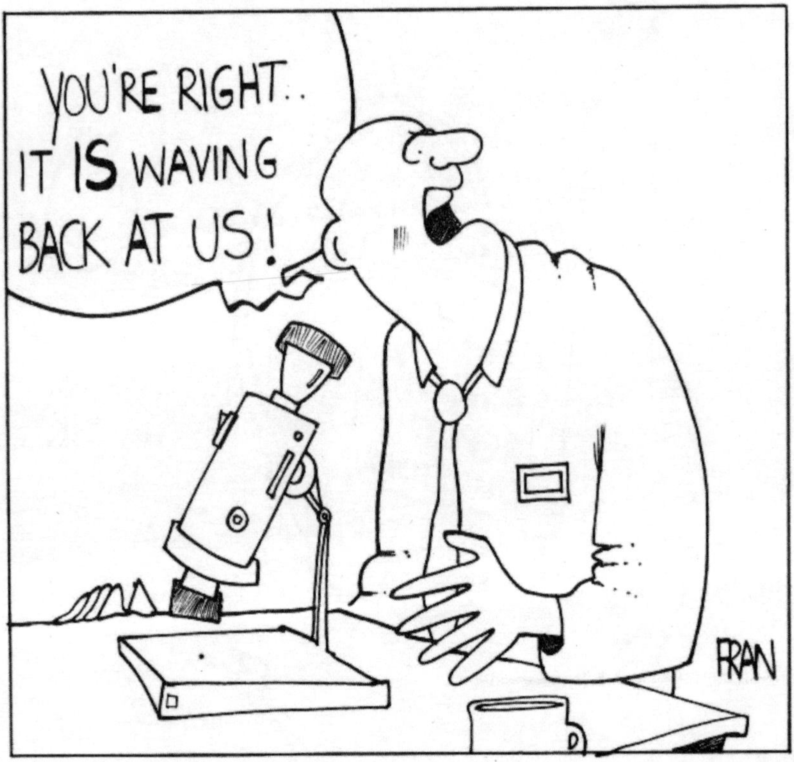
YOU'RE RIGHT..
IT IS WAVING
BACK AT US!
FRAN

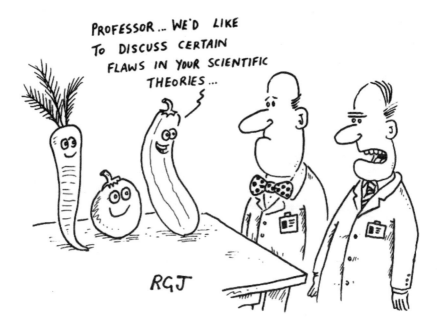

"Thats it. We've taken this genetic engineering too far"

Science

EUREKA...IT'S THE 'NATURAL' FLAVOUR WE'VE BEEN LOOKING FOR

INSULT

OF THE DAY

That woman speaks eight languages and can't say 'no' in any of them.

DOROTHY PARKER

JOKE OF THE DAY

What do a lawsuit and a viola have in common?
  Everyone is much happier when the case is closed.

Space and Aliens

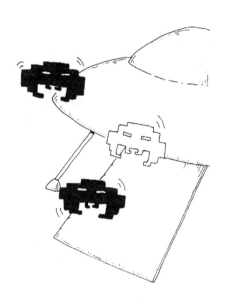

Space and Aliens

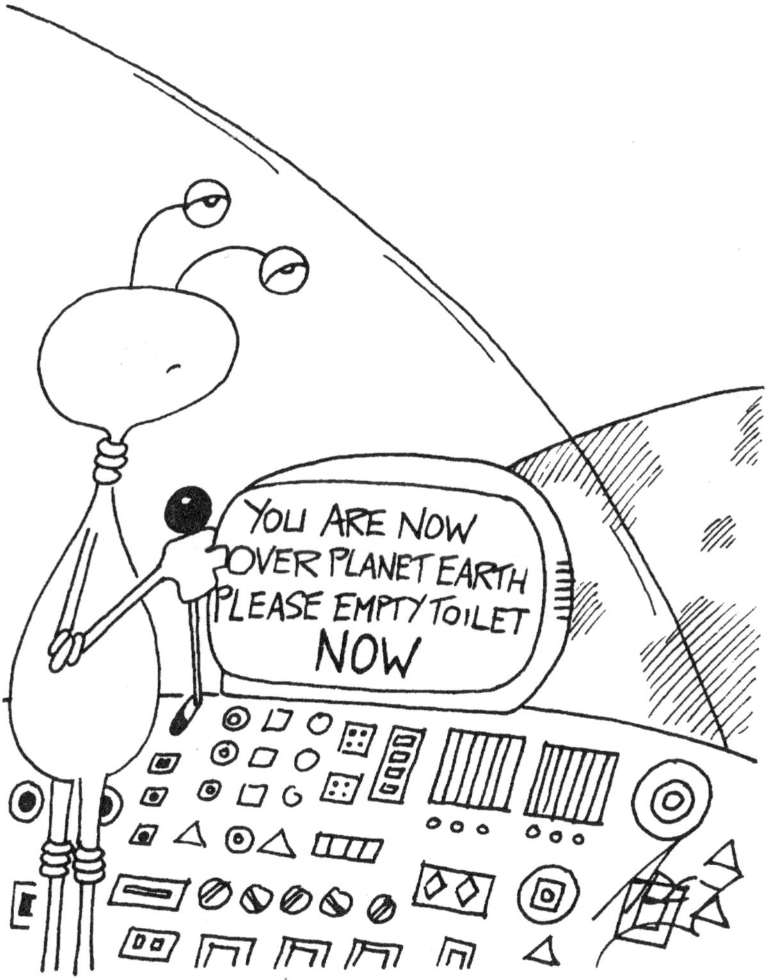

YOU ARE NOW
OVER PLANET EARTH
PLEASE EMPTY TOILET
NOW

Space and Aliens

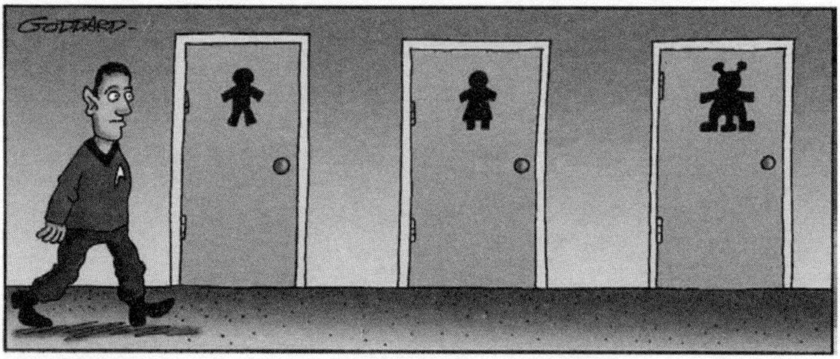
GODDARD

Space and Aliens

"Amazing Buzz! These moon rock samples you brought back in '69 contain evidence of water on the moon."

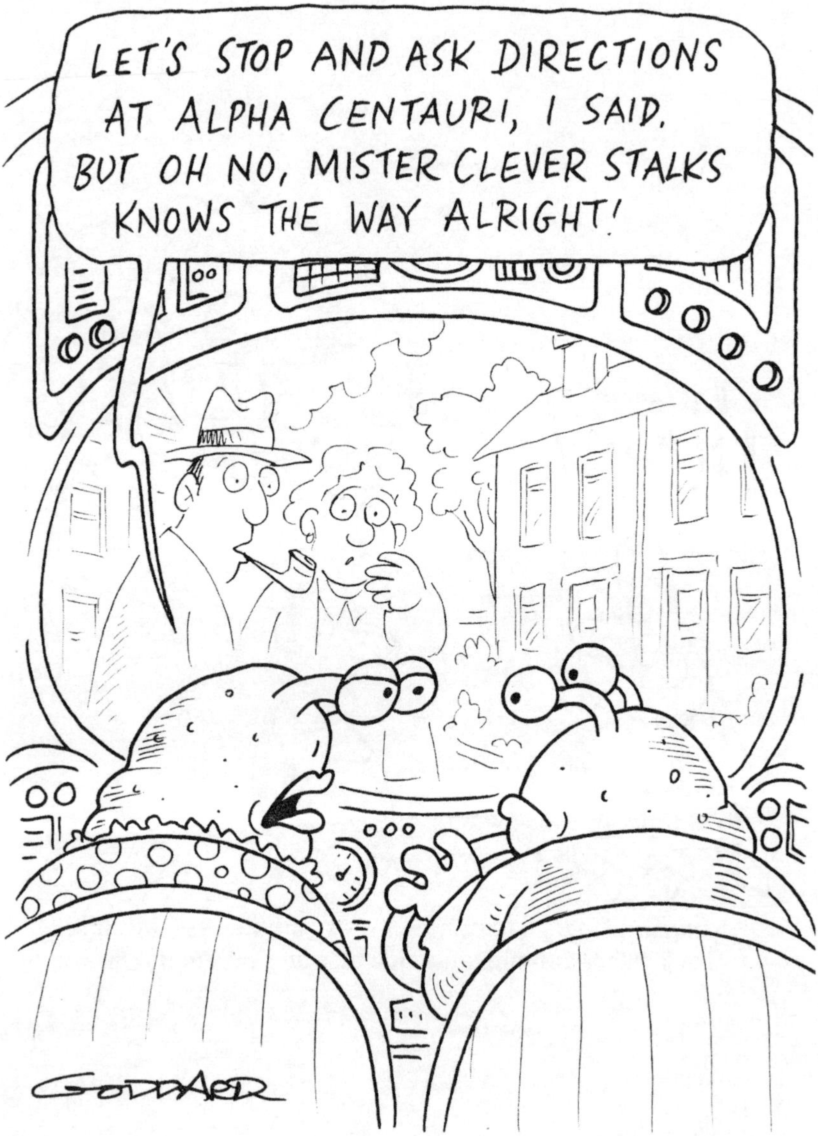
LET'S STOP AND ASK DIRECTIONS AT ALPHA CENTAURI, I SAID. BUT OH NO, MISTER CLEVER STALKS KNOWS THE WAY ALRIGHT!
GODDARD

Space and Aliens

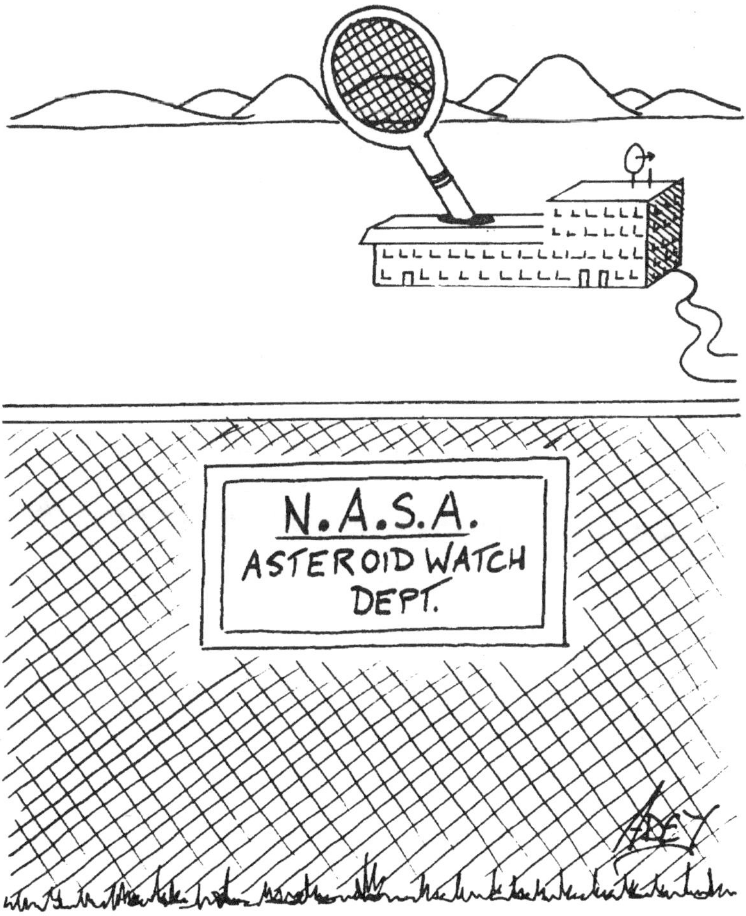
N.A.S.A.
ASTEROID WATCH
DEPT.

"Blimey, I thought I had a bad commute."

Space and Aliens

"I gave the human specimen some nourishment
and he blew a raspberry at me."

Space and Aliens

"I was expecting something a little more advanced."

Space and Aliens

GREAT EXCUSES NO. 964

" I was on my way to the gym when I was abducted by an alien from the planet Snarg who took me to their ship and force-fed me choc chip ice cream "

THOUGHT
FOR THE DAY

Some things, such as love or obligation, have meaning only if one stands to lose something by throwing them away.

INSULT
OF THE DAY

He hasn't an enemy in the world, but all his friends hate him.

JOKE OF THE DAY

A hole has appeared in the ladies' changing rooms at a local sports club. The police are looking into it.

Sports

Sports

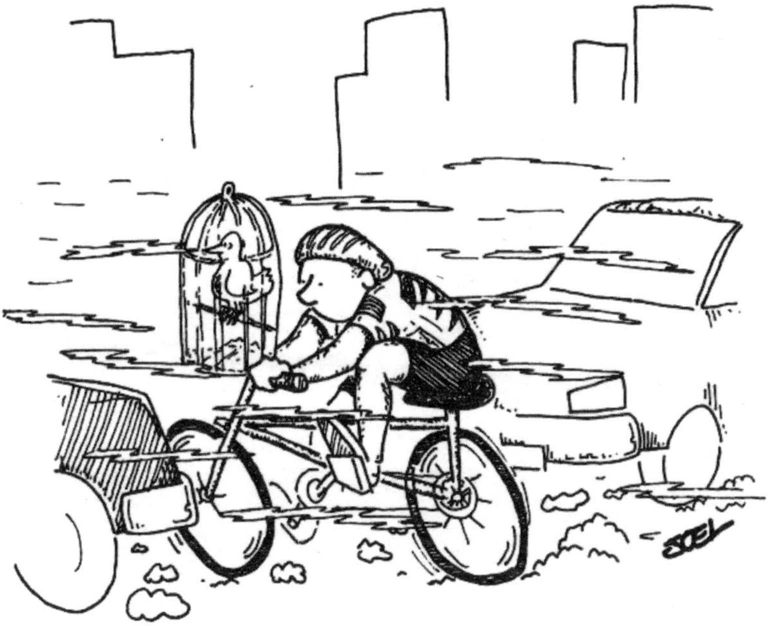
SOEL

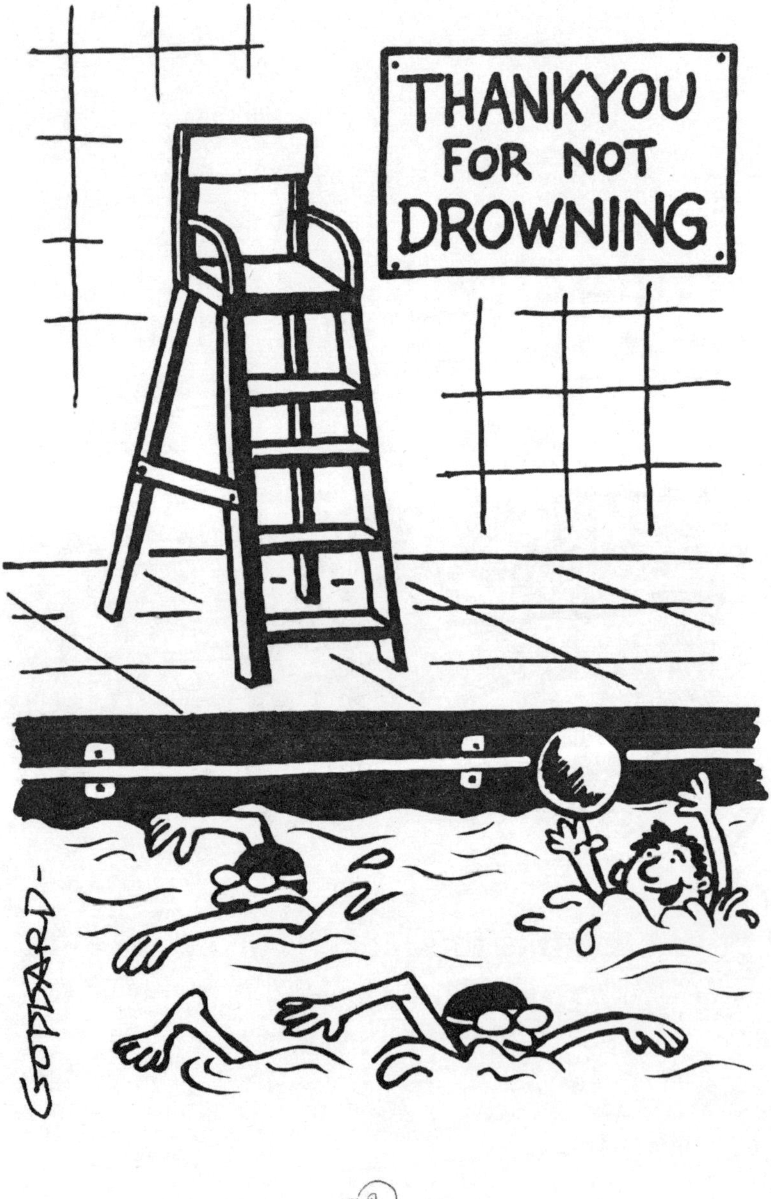
THANKYOU
FOR NOT
DROWNING
GODDARD

"I've been like this since I got back from my skiing holiday!"

"Thanks, we really appreciate this.
Yeah, the middle button. Don't worry,
it's auto-focus – just aim and shoot."

Sports

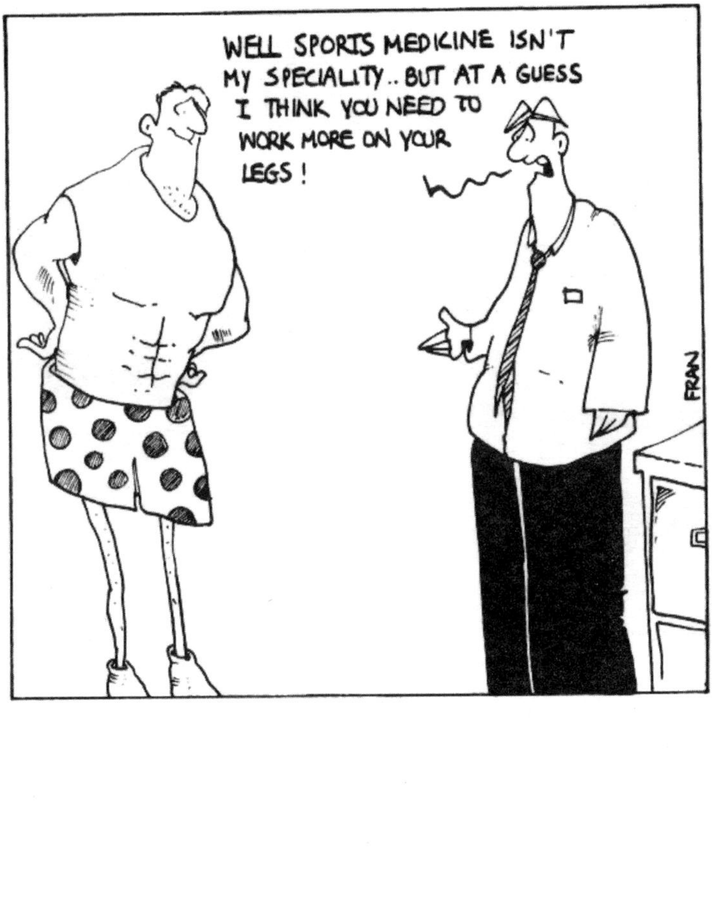
WELL SPORTS MEDICINE ISN'T MY SPECIALITY.. BUT AT A GUESS I THINK YOU NEED TO WORK MORE ON YOUR LEGS!
FRAN

Sports

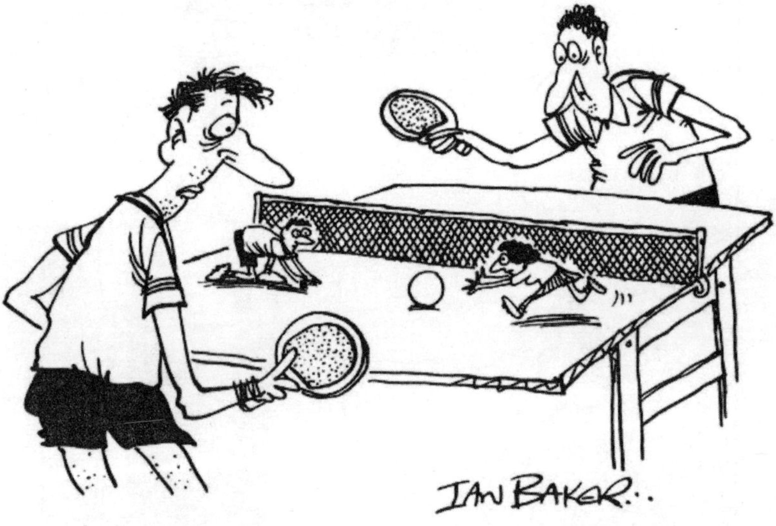
IAN BAKER...

"It was a mercy killing. I just couldn't stand to see him suffer in front of that TV each time his favorite team lost."

" The hare's demanding a dope test."

Sports

"I second the motion!"

INSULT
OF THE DAY

Some people don't hesitate to speak their minds because they have nothing to lose.

JOKE OF THE DAY

A plane was delayed for nearly an hour on take-off. When it eventually took to the air, the passengers asked the flight attendant the reason for the later departure.

'Well,' she explained, 'the pilot was worried about a noise he heard coming from one of the engines and it took us a while to get a new pilot.'

THOUGHT
FOR THE DAY

Other people are quite dreadful. The only possible society is oneself.

OSCAR WILDE

Television

Television

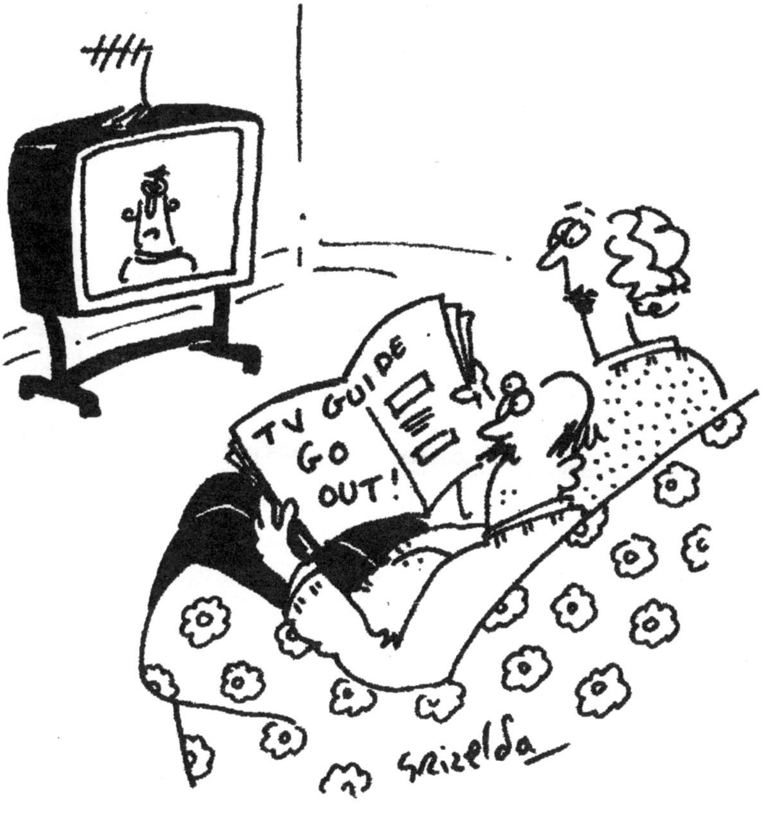
TV GUIDE
GO
OUT!
GRIZELDA

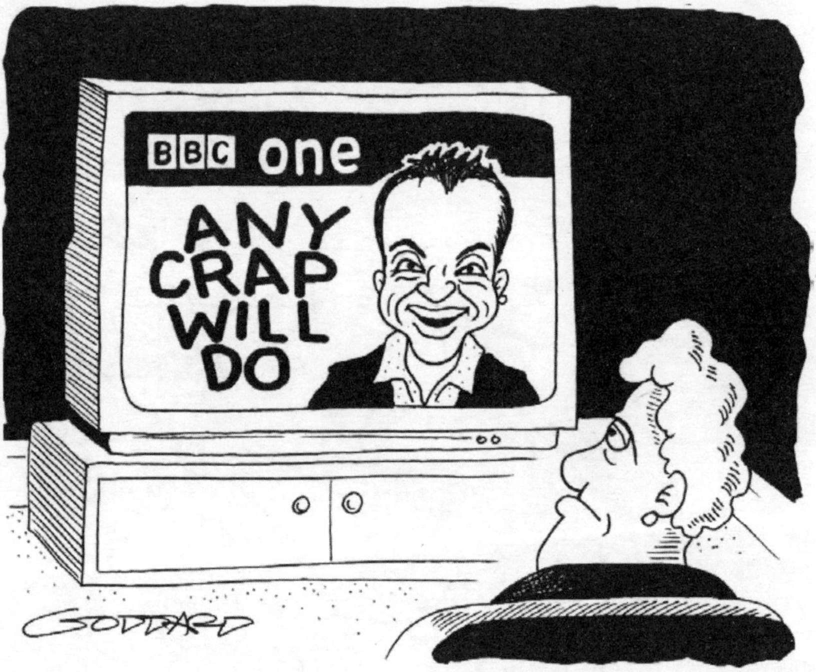
BBC one
ANY CRAP WILL DO
GODDARD

Television

"It's just toast I'm afraid, I've been
watching cookery programmes all evening."

Television

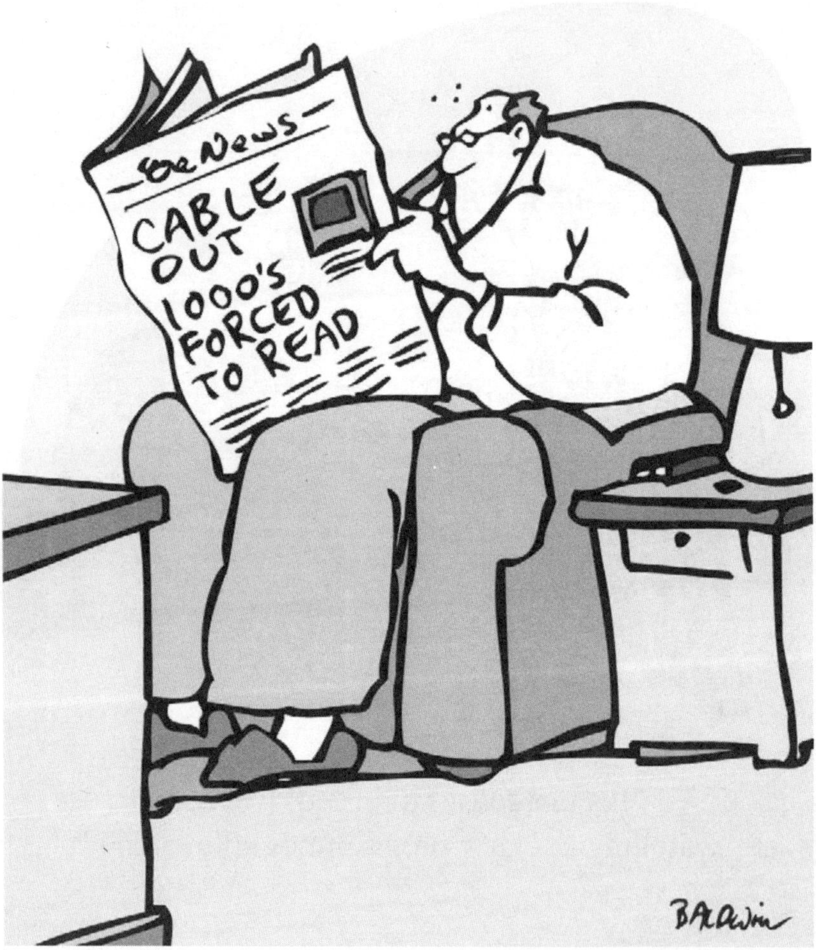
The News
CABLE OUT
1000's FORCED TO READ
BALDWIN

Television

"Move! You're blocking the TV."

Television

INSULT
OF THE DAY

He was a tubby little chap who looked like he had been poured into his clothes and forgotten to say 'when'.

P. G. WODEHOUSE

JOKE OF THE DAY

Two nuclear physicists got married recently. The ceremony was beautiful – she was absolutely radiant, and he was glowing, too. Even the bridesmaids shone.

THOUGHT
FOR THE DAY

One fool may maketh many.

Travel and Tourism

Travel and Tourism

"Does my bomb look big in this?"

Travel and Tourism

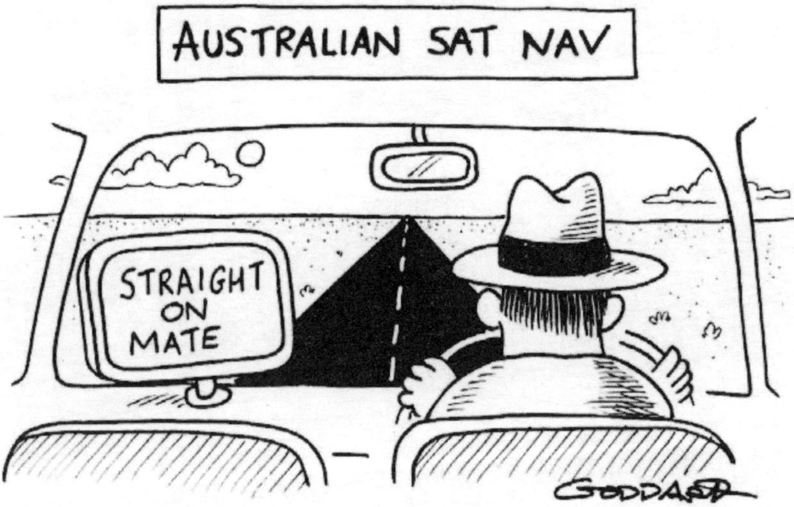
AUSTRALIAN SAT NAV
STRAIGHT ON MATE

Travel and Tourism

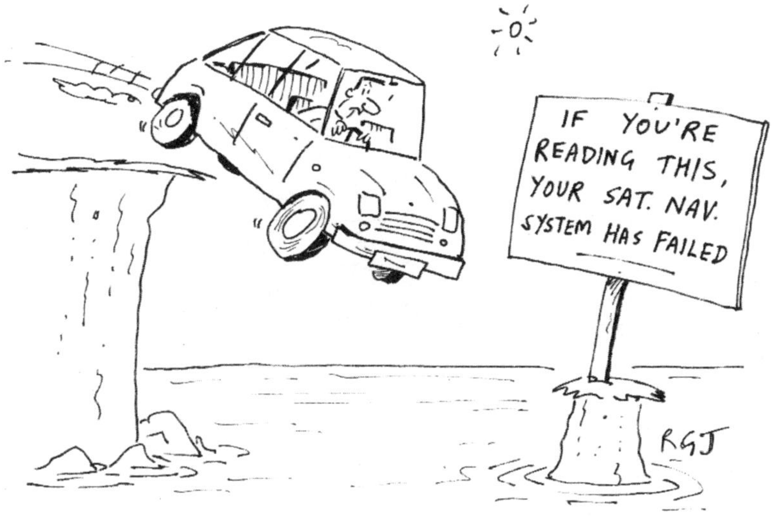
IF YOU'RE READING THIS, YOUR SAT. NAV. SYSTEM HAS FAILED
RGJ

Travel and Tourism

I CAN'T PUT MY FINGER ON IT PHILIP...BUT SINCE YOU CAME BACK
FROM THE SAFARI YOU'VE BEEN **DIFFERENT!**

"Wait, maybe it's, 'Keep your eyes on the road and your hands on the wheel.'"

Travel and Tourism

"Houston, contact a Mr. Malcolm Tadworth
of Sussex. I've found the luggage from
his 1987 holiday to Marbella."

Travel and Tourism

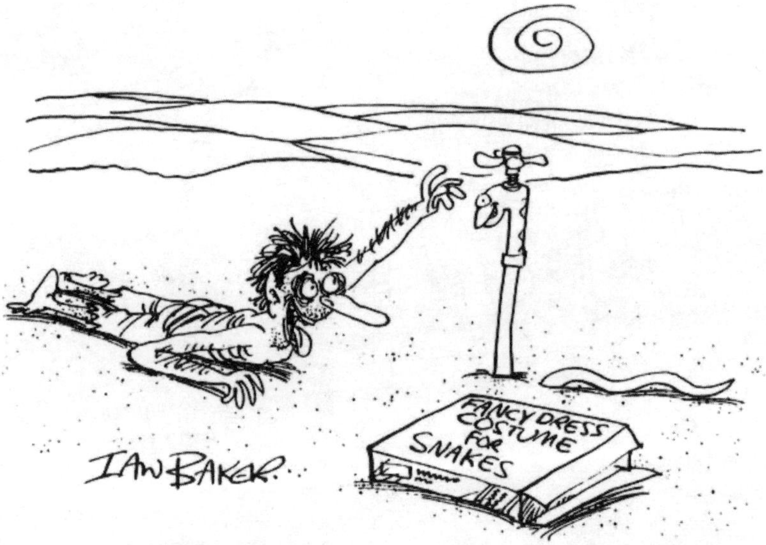
FANCY DRESS
COSTUME
FOR
SNAKES
IAN BAKER

Travel and Tourism

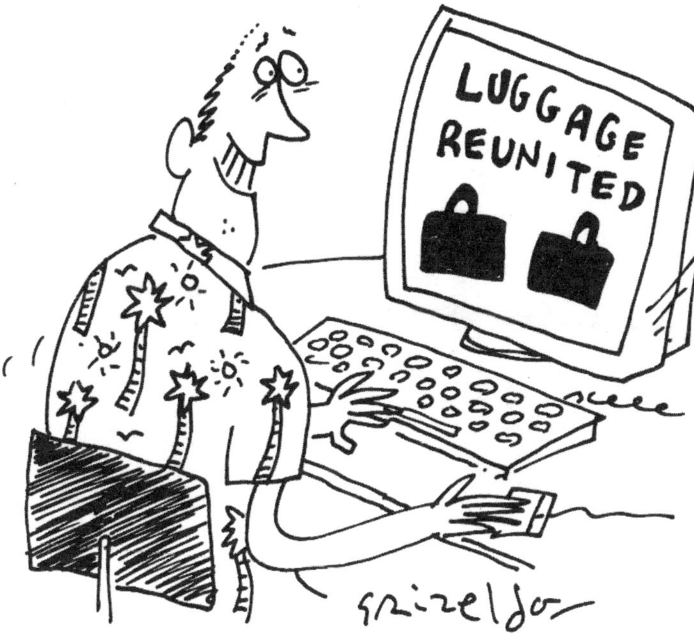
LUGGAGE
REUNITED

"You may find the mosquitos
around here a little tiresome"

Travel and Tourism

THE TIP OF THE ICEBERG

THOUGHT
FOR THE DAY

The enemy of your enemy is your friend.

JOKE OF THE DAY

Why don't actors stare out of the window in the morning?
  Because if they did, they'd have nothing to do in the afternoon.

THOUGHT
FOR THE DAY

Any fool can criticize,
condemn and complain
and most fools do.

BENJAMIN FRANKLIN

Credits

Ian Baker
14, 24, 43, 61, 76, 87, 123, 135, 143, 152, 189, 195, 228, 239, 263, 274, 304, 351, 354, 382.

Mike Baldwin
3, 7, 11, 13, 27, 41, 44, 62, 70, 77, 88, 95, 97, 99, 103, 109, 121, 124, 126, 137, 144, 153, 155, 159, 171, 192, 194, 201, 203, 205, 207, 209, 212, 218, 221, 230, 232, 240, 242, 249, 265, 273, 276, 287, 289, 298, 300, 303, 311, 313, 315, 316, 352, 355, 366, 368, 380.

Adey Bryant
5, 9, 16, 21, 25, 47, 55, 59, 64, 93, 102, 105, 110, 112, 114, 116, 117, 158, 164, 167, 175, 188, 190, 193, 204, 251, 261, 296, 299, 301, 324, 335, 339, 341, 384.

Credits

Clive Goddard
4, 10, 12, 22, 29, 36, 45, 56, 69, 71, 75, 82, 85, 94, 98, 122, 136, 150, 157, 166, 177, 187, 202, 206, 259, 272, 284, 295, 297, 305, 321, 323, 336, 338, 350, 364, 376.

Grizelda
15, 37, 42, 60, 74, 84, 86, 89, 96, 140, 142, 149, 154, 156, 196, 208, 211, 217, 219, 229, 250, 253, 262, 275, 363, 365, 383.

Richard Jolley
23, 26, 49, 57, 63, 101, 104, 113, 115, 163, 165, 168, 178, 191, 227, 231, 255, 260, 264, 267, 290, 325, 329, 337, 340, 375, 377, 381, 385.

Joel Mishon
6, 30, 58, 72, 81, 83, 125, 127, 129, 139, 141, 176, 180, 182, 238, 252, 266, 283, 285, 288, 302, 322, 327, 342, 349, 356, 378.

John Morris
35, 38, 40, 48, 128, 130, 138, 169, 179, 254, 326, 357.

Animals

Fran Orford
8, 28, 39, 46, 73, 100, 111, 151, 170, 181, 183, 210, 220, 222, 233, 237, 241, 243, 271, 277, 286, 291, 312, 314, 328, 330, 343, 353, 367, 369, 379.

—